A1

·Fast·Fast·Fast·

Phrasebook

Englisch
für
Erwachsene

First Choice

Cornelsen

First Choice A1 Fast Phrasebook

Redaktion	Sigrid Janssen Kathrin Köller
Redaktionelle Mitarbeit	Elizabeth Hine Christine House Marita Lampe
Projektleitung	Helga Holtkamp
Layout und technische Umsetzung	Oxford Designers & Illustrators Oliver Busch, Berlin
Umschlaggestaltung	Knut Waisznor
Umschlagfoto	ips, International Publishing Services für Cornelsen Verlag, © Cornelsen Verlag
Zum Lehrwerk gehören	**Kursbuch** mit **Phrasebook** und **Audio-CDs** **Teaching Guide** **Extra Language Trainer** mit **CD-ROM**

www.cornelsen.de

1. Auflage, 1. Druck 2005

Alle Drucke dieser Auflage sind inhaltlich unverändert und können im Unterricht nebeneinander verwendet werden.

Druck: CS-Druck CornelsenStürtz, Berlin

ISBN-13: 978-3-464-20208-1
ISBN-10: 3-464-20208-9

Inhalt gedruckt auf säurefreiem Papier,
umweltschonend hergestellt aus chlorfrei gebleichten Faserstoffen.

INHALT

HINWEISE ZUR BENUTZUNG

Im **First Choice A1 Fast Phrasebook** können Sie die Wörter, die im Kursbuch vorkommen, nachschlagen. Sie finden zu jedem Wort Hinweise zur Aussprache und die passende Übersetzung. Wenn ein Wort mehrere Bedeutungen hat, wird es so übersetzt, wie es in der Unit verwendet wird.

Das **First Choice A1 Fast Phrasebook** ist aber nicht nur ein nützliches Nachschlagewerk – Sie können damit auch selbstständig und effektiv lernen:

- Beispielsätze zeigen Ihnen, wie man das Wort benutzt, und geben Ihnen Aufschluss über die Satzstellung.
- Bei feststehenden Redewendungen haben wir die ganze Formulierung übersetzt, sodass Sie sofort den richtigen Ausdruck parat haben.
- Wörter und Wendungen, die thematisch zusammen gehören, lernen Sie in Wortfeldern.
- Die rosa Aufkleber geben zusätzliche Informationen und bewahren Sie vor typischen Fehlern.
- Zum Vokabellernen legen Sie einfach Ihr Lesezeichen mit der oberen Kante auf die Seite. Beispielsatz und englisches Wort sind verdeckt, sodass Sie sich ganz bequem selbst abfragen können.

Sie finden jedes Wort an der Stelle, an der es zum ersten Mal auftaucht. Sollten Sie ein Wort nachschlagen wollen, von dem Sie nicht wissen, wo es zum ersten Mal verwendet wurde, schauen Sie einfach in das alphabetische Register.

Viel Spaß beim Lernen mit Ihrem *Phrasebook*.

Verwendete Abkürzungen

Abk.	Abkürzung	jdn	jemanden	
AE	American English	Pl.	Plural	
BE	British English	sb	somebody	jemand/em/en
jd	jemand	sth	something	etwas
jdm	jemandem			

Hinweise zur Aussprache

ɑ: wie in **a**sk [ɑːsk]
ʌ wie in b**u**s [bʌs]
æ wie in c**a**n [kæn]
e wie in **e**ntertainment [ˌentə'teɪnmənt]
i: wie in h**e** [hiː]
i wie in happ**y** ['hæpi]
ɪ wie in s**i**t [sɪt]
ɜ: wie in b**i**rthday ['bɜːθdeɪ]
ɒ wie in g**o**t [gɒt]
ɔ: wie in sh**o**rts [ʃɔːts]
ʊ wie in b**oo**k [bʊk]
u: wie in f**oo**d [fuːd]
u wie in sit**u**ation [ˌsɪtʃu'eɪʃn]
ə wie in fath**er** ['fɑːðə]
aɪ wie in fl**i**ght [flaɪt]
aʊ wie in br**o**wse [braʊz]
eɪ wie in d**ate** [deɪt]
ɔɪ wie in b**oy** [bɔɪ]
ɪə wie in h**ea**r [hɪə]
eə wie in h**ai**r [heə]
əʊ wie in ph**o**ne [fəʊn]
ʊə wie in s**ure** [ʃʊə]
ŋ wie in darli**ng** ['dɑːlɪŋ]
s wie in **s**orry ['sɒri]
z wie in **z**ero ['zɪərəʊ]
ʃ wie in **sh**op [ʃɒp]
tʃ wie in **ch**icken ['tʃɪkɪn]
dʒ wie in **j**ob [dʒɒb]
v wie in **v**ideo['vɪdiəʊ]
r wie in **r**adio [ˌreɪdiəʊ]
ʒ wie in televi**si**on ['telɪvɪʒn]
θ wie in **th**ree [θriː]
ð wie in **th**is [ðɪs]
w wie in **w**onderful ['wʌndəfl]

First Choice

Unit word list

UNIT 1

Focus 1

first [ˌfɜːst]	erste/r/s	*the first English word*
contact [ˈkɒntækt]	Kontakt, Begegnung	*first contact*
(to) **meet sb** [ˈmiːt]	jdn treffen; jdn kennen lernen	*Nice to meet you.*
people [ˈpiːpl]	Leute, Menschen	
(to) **look at** [ˈlʊk ət]	ansehen, betrachten	*Look at the book.*
photo [ˈfəʊtəʊ]	Foto	*Look at the photos.*
(to) **read** [riːd]	lesen	*Read the text with a partner.*
dialogue [ˈdaɪəlɒg]	Dialog	*Read the dialogues.*
I'm (I am) [aɪm]	ich bin	*Hi, I'm Birgit.*
hello [həˈləʊ]	hallo	*"Hello! I'm your teacher."*
my [maɪ]	mein	*Hello, my name is Anna.*
name [neɪm]	Name	*My name's Claire.*
nice [naɪs]	nett, schön	*What a nice name!*
you [ju]	Sie, dich, euch	*Nice to meet you.*
this is … [ˈðɪs ɪz]	dies ist …	*This is Frank. – Nice to meet you, Frank.*
too [tuː]	auch	*Nice to meet you too.*
how [haʊ]	wie	*How are you?*
are [ɑː]	bist, sind, seid	*Her hobbies are squash and music.*
fine [faɪn]	gut, schön	*Fine, thanks.*
thanks [θæŋks]	danke	*Sandwich? – No, thanks.*

and [ənd]	und	*Tara and Steve are English.*
not [nɒt]	nicht	*I'm not from England, I'm from Scotland.*
bad [bæd]	schlecht	*How are you? – Not too bad, thank you.*
thank you ['θæŋk ju]	danke	*Your English is super. – Thank you.*
(to) **listen (to)** [lɪsn]	zuhören, anhören	*Listen to the CD.*
then [ðen]	dann	*Look at the photos, then read the text.*
them [ðem]	*3. Person Plural:* sie, ihnen	*Look at them.*
group [gru:p]	Gruppe	*Read the text in groups, please.*

Meeting people

My name's …	Ich heiße …
This is …	Dies ist …
Nice to meet you.	Schön, Sie/dich/euch kennen zu lernen.
Nice to meet you too.	Ich freue mich auch, Sie/dich/euch kennen zu lernen.
How are you?	Wie geht es Ihnen/dir?
Fine, thanks.	Danke, gut.
And you?	Und wie geht es Ihnen/dir/euch?
Not too bad, thank you.	Danke, auch ganz gut.

(to) **say** [seɪ]	sagen	*How do you say this in English?*
(to) **say hello to sb** [seɪ hə'ləʊ tə]	jdn begrüßen	
other ['ʌðə]	andere/r/s	*The other people in my class are nice.*
your [jɔ:]	Ihr/e, dein/e, euer/eure	*Say hello to your teacher.*
now [naʊ]	nun, jetzt	
(to) **tell sb sth** [tel]	jdm etwas sagen/erzählen	*Now tell the others about your hobbies.*
class [klɑ:s]	Klasse, Kurs	*Tell the class where you are from.*
about [ə'baʊt]	über	
(to) **complete** [kəm'pli:t]	vervollständigen	*Complete the dialogue, please.*
table ['teɪbl]	Tabelle	*Complete the table.*

he [hiː]	er	*He was born in Spain.*
single [ˈsɪŋgl]	allein stehend	*He's single.*
(to) **be born** [bi ˈbɔːn]	geboren sein	*She was born in Munich.*
journalist [ˈdʒɜːnəlɪst]	Journalist/in	*She's a journalist.*
magazine [ˌmægəˈziːn]	Magazin, Zeitschrift	*Read an English magazine.*
travel magazine [ˌtrævl ˌmægəˈziːn]	Reisemagazin	*He's a journalist for a travel magazine.*
from [frəm]	von, aus	*Are you from England?*
mother [ˈmʌðə]	Mutter	*My mother is a journalist.*
her [hɜː]	ihr	*Tara is from England. Her mother's Indian.*
father [ˈfɑːðə]	Vater	*My father's name is Bruno.*
… is English [ɪz ˈɪŋglɪʃ]	… ist Engländer/in	*Her father is English.*
computer expert [kəmˌpjuːtər ˈekspɜːt]	Computerexperte/ -expertin	*Tara's a computer expert.*
international [ˌɪntəˈnæʃnəl]	international	*English is international.*
hotel [həʊˈtel]	Hotel	*an international hotel*
hobby [ˈhɒbi]	Hobby	*My hobbies are music and sport.*
music [ˈmjuːzɪk]	Musik	
sport *(BE)* [spɔːt]	Sport	
job [dʒɒb]	Arbeit, Beruf	! What's your job? ~~My job is …~~ I'm a/an …
teacher [ˈtiːtʃə]	Lehrer/in	
she [ʃiː]	sie	*She's from Australia.*
ranch [rɑːntʃ]	Ranch, Rinderfarm	*He's an English teacher on a ranch.*
owner [ˈəʊnə]	Besitzer/in	*She's the owner of a bar.*
café [ˈkæfeɪ]	Café, Bistro	*She is the owner of the First Choice café.*
called [kɔːld]	namens, genannt	*I come from a town called Remagen.*

first choice [fɜːst ˈtʃɔɪs]	erste Wahl	*You are my first choice.*
there [ðeə]	da, dort	*See you there.*
super [ˈsuːpə]	super, toll	*The baby was born yesterday. – Oh, super!*
his [hɪz]	sein	*Peter? – His hobby is karaoke.*
karaoke [ˌkæriˈəʊki]	Karaoke	*His mother is a karaoke teacher.*
was [wɒz]	*Vergangenheitsform von* be, war	*My partner was born in London.*
taxi [ˈtæksi]	Taxi	*Where's the taxi?*
driver [ˈdraɪvə]	Fahrer/in	*He's a driver for an international hotel.*
but [bʌt]	aber	*The baguettes are nice, but the calories are bad.*
first name [ˈfɜːst neɪm]	Vorname	*My first name is Antje.*
surname [ˈsɜːneɪm]	Nachname	*What's your surname?*
yourself [jɔːˈself]	dich (selbst)	*Tell the others about yourself.*

Focus 2

word [wɜːd]	Wort	*Snack and jeans are international words.*
how many [ˌhaʊ ˈmenɪ]	wie viele	*How many people are in your group?*
can [kæn]	können	*Can I ask you something?*
(to) **find** [faɪnd]	finden	*Can you find the English words?*
exercise [ˈeksəsaɪz]	Übung, Aufgabe	*Read exercise three, please.*
these [ðiːz]	*Pl. von* this, diese	*How do you say these words?*
in English [ɪn ˈɪŋglɪʃ]	auf Englisch	*What is "Schokolade" in English?*
again [əˈgen]	wieder; noch einmal	*Nice to see you again.*
(to) **repeat** [rɪˈpiːt]	wiederholen	*Can you repeat that, please?*
(to) **make** [meɪk]	machen, anfertigen	*Can I make some tea?*
list [lɪst]	Liste	*Make a list of your hobbies.*

food [fuːd]	Essen, Nahrung(smittel)	*English food is super!*
drink [drɪŋk]	Getränk	*Can I have a drink, please?*
snack [snæk]	Imbiss	*A kebap is an international snack.*
spaghetti [spəˈgeti]	Spaghetti	*Oops! I have spaghetti on my top.*
snowboarding [ˈsnəʊbɔːdɪŋ]	Snowboarden	*Can you go snowboarding in Australia?*
fashion [ˈfæʃn]	Mode	
sweatshirt [ˈswetʃɜːt]	Sweatshirt	*The football team have special sweatshirts.*
travel [ˈtrævl]	Reisen	*last minute travel*
airport [ˈeəpɔːt]	Flughafen	*entertainment at the airport*
entertainment [ˌentəˈteɪnmənt]	Unterhaltung	! talk show (AE) chat show (BE)
talk show *(AE)* [ˈtɔːk ʃəʊ]	Talkshow	
cartoon [kɑːˈtuːn]	Cartoon; Zeichentrickfilm	
odd one out [ɒd wʌn ˈaʊt]	nicht dazugehörig	*3 is the odd one out in 2, 4, 6, 8.*
(to) **write** [raɪt]	schreiben	*Write me a postcard, please.*
more [mɔː]	weitere	*Write three more international words.*
item [ˈaɪtəm]	Ding, Gegenstand	*How many items can you see?*
(to) **give** [gɪv]	geben	*Give me the book, please.*
another [əˈnʌðə]	ein/e andere/r/s	*Give your list to another group.*
they [ðeɪ]	*3. Person Plural:* sie	
answer [ˈɑːnsə]	Antwort, Lösung	*Can you find the answer?*
hamburger [ˈhæmbɜːgə]	Hamburger	
sound card [ˈsaʊnd kɑːd]	Soundkarte	
pizza [ˈpiːtsə]	Pizza	*A pizza for me, please!*
volleyball [ˈvɒlibɔːl]	Volleyball	*Winston plays volleyball.*

team [ti:m]	Mannschaft	
shorts [ʃɔ:ts]	kurze Hose, Shorts	
word spider ['wɜ:d ˌspaɪdə]	Wortnetz	

! Shorts und jeans sind immer Plural im Englischen. Where are my jeans?

Focus 3

number ['nʌmbə]	(Telefon-)Nummer	*Can you give me your number?*
way [weɪ]	Weg	*The VHS is on my way to work.*
(to) **be on your way** [ɒn jɔ: 'weɪ]	unterwegs sein	*I'm on my way to see you.*
phone call ['fəʊn kɔ:l]	Anruf, Telefongespräch	*Ben misses his bus because of the phone call.*
(to) **tick** [tɪk]	abhaken, ankreuzen	*Tick the answer.*
sentence ['sentəns]	Satz	*Repeat the sentence, please.*
(to) **hear** [hɪə]	hören	*Hello …? Can you hear me?*
darling ['dɑ:lɪŋ]	Liebling, Schatz	*Bye, darling.*
happy ['hæpɪ]	glücklich, fröhlich	
birthday ['bɜ:θdeɪ]	Geburtstag	*Happy birthday!*
Pardon? ['pɑ:dn]	Wie bitte?	*Pardon? Can you say that again, please?*
it's me [ɪts 'mi:]	ich bin's	*Hello, it's me!*
check-in [ˌtʃek'ɪn]	Abfertigung(sschalter)	*Tara's at the check-in.*
Sorry! ['sɒri]	Tut mir Leid! Entschuldigung!	
wrong [rɒŋ]	falsch	*No, sorry, wrong answer.*
wrong number [rɒŋ 'nʌmbə]	falsch verbunden	*Oh sorry, I must have the wrong number!*
must [mʌst]	müssen	*You must be Laura. – Hello. Nice to meet you.*
(to) **have** [hæv]	haben	*I have two computers.*
You must have the wrong number.	Sie müssen sich verwählt haben.	
no problem [nəʊ 'prɒbləm]	kein Problem	

Don't worry. [dəʊnt 'wʌri]	Machen Sie sich/ Mach dir keine Sorgen.	*Don't worry. Be happy.*
phone number ['fəʊn ˌnʌmbə]	Telefonnummer	*What's your phone number?*
which [wɪtʃ]	welche/r/s	
mobile number *(BE)* ['məʊbaɪl ˌnʌmbə]	Mobilnummer	*Can I have your mobile number?*
cellphone *(AE)* ['selfəʊn]	Handy	*Is it your cellphone number?*
(to) **mean** [mi:n]	bedeuten	*What does this mean?*
something ['sʌmθɪŋ]	etwas	*Can I ask you something?*
(to) **ask** [ɑ:sk]	fragen	*Ask and answer.*
(to) **answer** ['ɑ:nsə]	antworten	*Can you answer the question?*
(to) **find out** ['faɪnd aʊt]	herausfinden	*Find out what your partner's hobbies are.*
what [wɒt]	was	*What are your hobbies?*
it [ɪt]	es	*Is it your mobile number? – Yes, it is.*
house ['haʊs]	Haus	*Our house is in Lincoln.*
house number ['haʊs 'nʌmbə]	Hausnummer	*What's his house number?*
yes [jes]	ja	*Is your name Sue? – Yes, it is.*
no [nəʊ]	nein	*Are you Jim? – No, I'm John.*

Magazine

doctor ['dɒktə]	Arzt/Ärztin	*Ann is a doctor.*
where [weə]	wo, woher	*Where are you from?*
What's your name?	Wie heißen Sie / heißt du?	
reporter [rɪ'pɔ:tə]	Reporter/in	*I'm a TV reporter.*
footballer ['fʊtbɔ:lə]	Fußballspieler/in	*She's a footballer.*
restaurant ['restrɒnt]	Restaurant	*Is it an English restaurant?*
book [bʊk]	Buch	*Is that a good book?*

first contact

What's your name?	Wie heißen Sie? / Wie heißt du?
My name's ...	Ich heiße …
Where are you from?	Woher kommen Sie? / Woher kommst du?
I'm from ...	Ich komme aus …
It's nice to be here.	Schön, hier zu sein.
How do you do?	Angenehm, Sie kennen zu lernen./ Guten Tag/Abend.

meeting [mˈiːtɪŋ]	Treffen, Besprechung	*I'm sorry, she's in a meeting.*
early [ˈɜːli]	früh	*The flight is early.*
flight [flaɪt]	Flug	*The flight is at 6.00.*
(to) **see** [siː]	sehen	
later [ˈleɪtə]	später	*Can I see you later?*
See you later!	Bis nachher!	*See you later, alligator!*
expert [ˈekspɜːt]	Experte, Expertin	
greetings [ˈgriːtɪŋz]	Grüße	*Greetings to Gary.*
(to) **match** [mætʃ]	zuordnen	*Match the photos, please.*
picture [ˈpɪktʃə]	Bild	*What's in the picture?*
our [aʊə]	unser	*She's from our Munich office.*
office [ˈɒfɪs]	Büro	*I'm from the London office.*
welcome (to) [ˈwelkəm tə]	willkommen (bei)	*Welcome to First Choice.*
(to) **be** [biː]	sein	*"To be or not to be …"*
here [hɪə]	hier	*Hello, I'm here.*
great [greɪt]	groß(artig), toll	*The food is great.*
delicious [dɪˈlɪʃəs]	köstlich	*This is delicious.*
by the way [baɪ ðə ˈweɪ]	übrigens	*I'm Tara, by the way.*
(to) **do** [duː]	tun, machen	*What do you do? – I'm a doctor.*

Story

story ['stɒrɪ]	Geschichte	*That was a great story!*
bye ['baɪ]	Tschüss	*Bye! See you in the restaurant.*
often ['ɒfn]	oft, häufig	*I often meet Tara.*
(to) **be away** [ˌbiː ə'weɪ]	weg/unterwegs sein	*I'm often away in August.*
business ['bɪznəs]	Geschäft, Firma	*This is my mother's business.*
on business [ɒn 'bɪznəs]	dienstlich, geschäftlich	*Tara is often away on business.*
today [tə'deɪ]	heute	*She is in Paris today.*
(to) **have a meeting** [ˌhəv ə 'miːtɪŋ]	eine Besprechung haben	*Sarah has a meeting in Berlin.*
very ['veri]	sehr	*My bus is very late.*
(to) **phone** [fəʊn]	anrufen, telefonieren	*Tara phones Steve.*
(to) **take a taxi** (to) [teɪk ə 'tæksi]	ein Taxi nehmen	*She takes a taxi to her hotel.*
company ['kʌmpəni]	Unternehmen, Firma	*The company is in Munich.*
Damn! [dæm]	Verdammt!	*Damn! I'm late for my English class!*
(to) **miss** [mɪs]	verpassen	*Our teacher missed the bus too.*
bus [bʌs]	(Linien-)Bus	*Ben is on the bus from London to Oxford.*
because of [bɪ'kɒz əv]	wegen, aufgrund von	*I can't come because of my job.*
late [leɪt]	spät	! Sorry, I'm late. ~~Sorry, I'm too late.~~
(to) **be late** [bi 'leɪt]	(zu) spät kommen	
phrase [freɪz]	(Rede-)Wendung	
week [wiːk]	Woche	*Have a nice week! – And you.*

Have a nice evening! — Einen schönen Abend!

Thanks. You too. — Danke, Ihnen/dir auch.

UNIT 2

Focus 1

(to) **keep** [ki:p]	bleiben	*Keep in contact!*
(to) **check** [tʃek]	überprüfen	*Please check your answers.*
game [geɪm]	Spiel	*Play the game.*
(to) **look round** [ˌlʊk 'raʊnd]	sich umsehen	*Look round the class.*
(to) **remember** [rɪ'membə]	sich erinnern (an)	*I can't remember your name.*
student ['stju:dnt]	Schüler/in; Student/in	! Students gibt es nicht nur an der Universität. Wenn man z. B. an der VHS lernt, ist man auch a student.
(to) **introduce oneself** [ˌɪntrə'dju:s]	sich vorstellen	
(to) **test** [test]	prüfen, testen	
(to) **think** [θɪŋk]	glauben, denken, meinen	
right [raɪt]	richtig	*I think that's right.*
positive ['pɒzətɪv]	bejahend, positiv	*Give me a positive answer, please.*
negative ['negətɪv]	verneinend, negativ	*Please write a negative sentence.*
question ['kwestʃən]	Frage	*Can I ask you a question?*
short form ['ʃɔ:t fɔ:m]	Kurzform	*What's the short form of "I am"?*
right [raɪt]	nicht wahr	*You're Sarah, right?*
guest [gest]	Gast	*They aren't nice guests.*
(to) **choose** ['tʃu:z]	wählen, auswählen	*Choose the right word.*
some [sʌm]	einige, etwas; *wird oft nicht übersetzt*	*There are some interesting things to see.*
below [bɪ'ləʊ]	unten	*Look at the sentence below.*
good [gʊd]	gut	*Have a good weekend.*
morning ['mɔ:nɪŋ]	Morgen, Vormittag	*Good morning. How are you?*
(to) **help** [help]	helfen	*Can I help you?*

What was your name again?	Wie war nochmal Ihr Name?	
reservation [ˌrezəˈveɪʃn]	Reservierung	*My name is Smith. I have a reservation.*
night [naɪt]	Nacht	*I write books at night.*
double (room) [ˌdʌbl ˈruːm]	Doppelzimmer	*Can I have a double room, please?*
single (room) [ˌsɪŋgl ˈruːm]	Einzelzimmer	*A single for two nights, please.*
smoker [ˈsməʊkə]	Raucher-	*She's a smoker.*
non-smoker [ˌnɒnˈsməʊkə]	Nichtraucher-	*Her partner is a non-smoker.*
(to) **show** [ʃəʊ]	zeigen	*Could you show me how to do this?*
me [miː]	mir, mich	*Can you write it for me?*
passport [ˈpɑːspɔːt]	(Reise-)Pass	
please [pliːz]	bitte	
Here you are. [hɪə ju ˈɑː]	Bitte(schön).	
(to) **practise** [ˈpræktɪs]	üben	
with [wɪð]	mit	
(to) **act out sth** [ækt ˈaʊt]	etwas vorspielen	*Can you act out the dialogue?*

!
Wenn Sie etwas haben möchten, sagen Sie please, wenn Sie jdm etwas geben: Here you are.

Focus 2

(to) **spell** [spel]	buchstabieren	*Can you spell your name, please?*
detail [ˈdiːteɪl]	Angabe	*Can you give me your contact details, please?*
(to) **circle** [ˈsɜːkl]	einkreisen	*Circle the right answer.*
letter [ˈletə]	Buchstabe	*How many letters are in the word letter? – 6.*
or [ɔː]	oder	*Is your name Karin or Kathrin?*
(to) **send** [send]	senden, schicken	*Send a message to your darling.*
this [ðɪs]	diese/r/s	*Is this your credit card?*
message [ˈmesɪdʒ]	Nachricht	*Is there no message for me?*

text (message) ['tekst ˌmesɪdʒ]	SMS	*Please send me a text.*
work [wɜːk]	Arbeit	*I love my work.*
(to) **be at work** [bi ət 'wɜːk]	auf/bei der Arbeit sein	*Are you at work?*
weekend [ˌwiːk'end]	Wochenende	*See you at the weekend.*
telephone ['telɪfəʊn]	Telefon	*I can't find my telephone.*
conversation [ˌkɒnvə'seɪʃn]	Gespräch, Unterhaltung	*Listen to a conversation in English.*
reception (desk) [rɪ'sepʃn desk]	Rezeption	*She asks for a room at the reception desk.*
desk [desk]	(Schreib-)Tisch	
(to) **fill in** [ˌfɪl 'ɪn]	ausfüllen, eintragen	
information [ˌɪnfə'meɪʃn]	Information(en)	

(!) Information ist im Englischen immer Singular.

fax [fæks]	Fax	**check-out date** [tʃek'aʊt deɪt]	Abreisedatum
email ['iːmeɪl]	E-Mail	**credit card** [kredɪt ˌkɑːd]	Kreditkarte
passport ['pɑːspɔːt]	(Reise-)Pass	**payment** ['peɪmənt]	Zahlung
passport number ['pɑːspɔːt ˌnʌmbə]	Passnummer	**exp.** [ɪk'spaɪə]	*Abk. von* expire, ablaufen
date of birth [ˌdeɪt əv 'bɜːθ]	Geburtsdatum	**security code** [sɪ'kjʊərəti kəʊd]	Sicherheitscode
check-in date [tʃek'ɪn deɪt]	Ankunftsdatum		

TRANSCRIPT

What's the name, please?	Wie heißen Sie, bitte?	
that [ðæt]	dies/e/r	*Can you give me that book there?*
also ['ɔːlsəʊ]	auch	*I like holidays but I also like staying at home.*
(to) **guarantee** [ˌgærən'tiː]	garantieren	*Can you guarantee you love me? – No.*
different ['dɪfrənt]	verschieden, unterschiedlich	*Practise the dialogue with different names, please.*
address [ə'dres]	Adresse	*What's your email address?*

www [ˌdʌbljuː dʌbljuː ˈdʌbljuː]	World Wide Web	**/ = slash** [slæʃ]	*Symbol für* slash, Schrägstrich, slash
mail [meɪl]	*Abk. von* email, Mail	**com** [kɒm]	*Abk. von* company: *E-Mail-Adresse eines Unternehmens*
@ = at [æt]	bei, at	**au = Australia** [ɒˈstreɪliə]	Australien
. = dot [dɒt]	Punkt, dot	**uk = United Kingdom** [ˌjuː ˈkeɪ]	Vereinigtes Königreich
- = hyphen [ˈhaɪfn]	minus	**in one word** [ɪn wʌn ˈwɜːd]	zusammen-geschrieben
_ = underscore [ˈʌndəˌskɔː]	Unterstrich		

if [ɪf]	wenn, falls	*Give me your email address – if you have one.*
one [ˈwʌn]	eine/r/s	
(to) **walk** [wɔːk]	(zu Fuß) gehen	*She walks to work.*
only [ˈəʊnli]	nur	*It's only you I love.*

In class

Can you repeat that, please?	Können Sie/Kannst du das bitte wiederholen?
Can you spell that?	Können Sie/Kannst du das buchstabieren?
OK, I've got that.	Gut, das habe ich (notiert).
Walk round the class.	Gehen Sie/Geht in der Klasse herum.

Magazine

writer [ˈraɪtə]	Schriftsteller/in	*Joanne K. Rowling is a writer.*
actress [ˈæktrəs]	Schauspielerin	*Is she an actress? – No, she isn't.*
singer [ˈsɪŋə]	Sänger/in	*She's a singer in a band.*
actor [ˈæktə]	Schauspieler	*Brad Pitt is an actor.*
model [ˈmɒdl]	Model, Fotomodell	*He's a model.*
politician [ˌpɒləˈtɪʃn]	Politiker/in	*She's a politician.*

coffee ['kɒfi]	Kaffee	*The coffee in Serena's café is very good.*
tea [tiː]	Tee	

course [kɔːs]	Kurs, Lehrgang	**month** [mʌnθ]	Monat
registration form [ˌredʒɪ'streɪʃn fɔːm]	Anmeldeformular	**year** [jɪə]	Jahr
school [skuːl]	Schule	**occupation** [ˌɒkju'peɪʃn]	Beruf, Tätigkeit
personal details [ˌpɜːsənl 'diːteɪlz]	persönliche Angaben	(to) **attach** [ə'tætʃ]	anbringen
family name ['fæməli neɪm]	Familienname	**recent** ['riːsnt]	aktuell
nationality [ˌnæʃə'næləti]	Staatsangehörigkeit	**contact address** [ˌkɒntækt ə'dres]	Kontaktadresse
title ['taɪtl]	Titel	**street** [striːt]	Straße
Mr ['mɪstə]	Herr	**town** [taʊn]	Stadt
Mrs ['mɪsɪz]	Frau *verheiratet*	**post code** ['pəʊst kəʊd]	Postleitzahl
Ms [mɪz]	Frau *neutrale Form*	**country** ['kʌntri]	Land; Staat
Miss [mɪs]	Fräulein *veraltet*	**telephone** ['telɪfəʊn]	Telefon
gender ['dʒendə]	Geschlecht	**identity card** [aɪ'dentəti kɑːd]	(Personal-) Ausweis
male [meɪl]	männlich, Männer-	**identity card number**	Ausweisnummer
female ['fiːmeɪl]	weiblich, Frauen-	**signature** ['sɪgnətʃə]	Unterschrift
mother tongue ['mʌðə tʌŋ]	Muttersprache	**date** [deɪt]	Datum
day [deɪ]	Tag		

Story

before [bɪ'fɔː]	bevor	*Before you go – what's for homework?*
(to) **leave** [liːv]	weggehen; verlassen	*Tara leaves Paris.*
(to) **go** [gəʊ]	gehen, fahren	*Can you go?*
wine [waɪn]	Wein	*Before she leaves, Tara buys some wine.*

shop [ʃɒp]	Geschäft, Laden	*I have summer job in my father's shop.*
wine shop ['waɪn ʃɒp]	Weinhandlung	*Before she leaves, Tara goes to a wine shop.*
(to) **buy** [baɪ]	kaufen	*Ben buys an English book.*
bottle [bɒtl]	Flasche	*A bottle of champagne, please.*
champagne [ʃæm'peɪn]	Champagner	*Champagne for me, please.*
when [wen]	wenn; als; wann	*When I see you, I'm happy.*
(to) **arrive** [ə'raɪv]	ankommen, eintreffen	*He arrives home early.*
home [həʊm]	zu Hause	
(to) **give** [gɪv]	schenken	
can't [kɑːnt]	*verneinte Form von* can, nicht können	
(to) **celebrate** ['selɪbreɪt]	feiern	*I can't celebrate my birthday this year.*
together [tə'geðə]	zusammen	*Tara and Steve can't celebrate his birthday together.*
evening ['iːvnɪŋ]	Abend	*See you in the evening.*
band [bænd]	Band	*Tara is in a band.*
its [ɪts]	sein/e, ihr/e	*The band has its concert in April.*
practice session ['præktɪs seʃn]	Übungsstunde	*It's my practice session today.*
because [bɪ'kɒz]	weil	*They can't meet because Tara's away on business.*
gig [gɪg]	*bei Unterhaltungsmusik:* Konzert, Auftritt	*Her band has a gig.*

! (to) be at home = zu Hause sein
(to) go home = nach Hause gehen

Nice to see you again. Did you have a good week?

Schön, Sie/dich wieder zu sehen. Hatten Sie/Hattest du eine gute Woche?

Yes, thanks. And you?

Danke ja. Und Sie/du?

UNIT 3

TRANSCRIPT

Focus 1

life [laɪf]	Leben	*She has a happy life.*
who [hu:]	wer	*Who is on the phone?*
phone [fəʊn]	Telefon	*Where's the phone?*
(to) **ring** [rɪŋ]	klingeln	*The phone rings. Can you anwer it?*
colleague ['kɒli:g]	Kollege/Kollegin	
boss [bɒs]	Chef/in	
What's the problem? ['wɒts ðə ˌprɒbləm]	Wo liegt das Problem?	
the second time [ðə 'sekənd taim]	das zweite Mal	*This is the second time you're late.*
this week [ðɪs wi:k]	diese Woche	*This week is a good week.*
correct [kə'rekt]	richtig	*Tick the correct answer.*
(to) **be on the phone**	am Telefon sein	*Your mother is on the phone.*
Today is not his day.	Heute ist nicht sein Tag.	

!
boss = Chef
chef = Küchenchef

Focus 2

(to) **talk about sth** ['tɔ:k əˌbaʊt]	über etwas sprechen	*She talks about her job all day long.*
family ['fæməli]	Familie	*This is my family.*
(to) **worry** ['wʌri]	sich Sorgen machen	*Don't worry!*
… isn't it? ['ɪzntɪt]	… nicht wahr?	*It's a great party, isn't it?*
That's you, isn't it?	Das sind Sie, nicht wahr? / Das bist du, oder?	
brother ['brʌðə]	Bruder	*This is my brother Tony.*
wedding ['wedɪŋ]	Hochzeit	*Look, that's me, at my brother's wedding.*
last [lɑ:st]	letzte/r/s	*My last bus is at 9.00.*
all [ɔ:l]	alle	*All these people are my friends.*
member ['membə]	Mitglied	*My brother is a member of my family.*

big [bɪg]	groß	*Wow, what a big party!*
well [wel]	nun, na ja	*Well, I'll go home.*
wife [waɪf]	Ehefrau	*She's my sister's wife.*
(to) **work (for sb)** [wɜːk]	für jdn arbeiten	*He works for his father.*
airline ['eəlaɪn]	Fluggesellschaft	*She works for an airline company.*
parents ['peərənts]	Eltern	*And these are your parents, right?*
sister ['sɪstə]	Schwester	*My sister is an actress.*
beautiful ['bjuːtɪfl]	(wunder)schön	*Wow, she's beautiful.*
husband ['hʌzbənd]	Ehemann	*This is my husband, Jack!*
their [ðeə]	ihr/e	*He's their son.*
son [sʌn]	Sohn	*I love my son.*
(to) **close** [kləʊz]	(ver)schließen	*Close your books, please.*
friend [frend]	Freund/in	*You're my best friend.*
(the) **same** [seɪm]	der, die, das gleiche	*My sister and I live in the same city.*
(to) **come from …** [kʌm frəm]	aus … kommen	*I come from Soest. Where do you come from?*
(to) **be married** [bi 'mærid]	verheiratet sein	*Winston is married and has two children.*
child, children [tʃaɪld, 'tʃɪldrən]	Kind, Kinder	*Jamaila has one child, her brother has two children.*
girl [gɜːl]	Mädchen	*The girl in the photo is her granddaughter.*
boy [bɔɪ]	Junge	*Is it a boy or a girl?*
unusual [ʌn'juːʒuəl]	ungewöhnlich	*What an unusual story!*
animal ['ænɪml]	Tier	*My son loves animals.*
therapist ['θerəpɪst]	Therapeut/in	*His partner is a therapist.*
(to) **live** [lɪv]	wohnen, leben	*She lives in England.*
grandparents ['grænpeərənts]	Großeltern	*Which grandparents? – My mother's parents.*

ex-wife [eks'waɪf]	Ex-Frau	*Look, there's your ex-wife.*
nephew ['nefjuː]	Neffe	*Denzel is my ex-wife's nephew.*
professional [prə'feʃənl]	professionell, hauptberuflich	*My brother is a professional squash player.*
tennis player ['tenɪs ˌpleɪə]	Tennisspieler/in	
(to) **play** [pleɪ]	spielen	*Can you play tennis?*
well [wel]	*Adverb von* good	*How well do you know your teacher?*
(to) **like** ['laɪk]	mögen, gern haben	*She likes chocolate.*
much [mʌtʃ]	sehr	*I don't like German food much.*
very much [ˌveri 'mʌtʃ]	sehr	
near ['nɪə]	nahe	! She lives near Frankfurt. ~~She lives in the near of Frankfurt.~~
friendly ['frendli]	freundlich, freundschaftlich	
almost ['ɔːlməʊst]	fast, beinahe	*I almost missed my flight yesterday.*
new [njuː]	neu	*She has a new boss.*
bank [bæŋk]	Bank	*My mother works for a bank.*
daughter ['dɔːtə]	Tochter	*Her daughter works for an international bank.*
verb [vɜːb]	Verb	*Choose the right verb.*
person ['pɜːsn]	*Sing. von* people, Mensch, Person	*She's a nice person.*
board [bɔːd]	Tafel	*Write the words on the board, please.*
someone ['sʌmwʌn]	jemand	*Hey, there's someone I know.*
(to) **know** [nəʊ]	kennen	*Do you know a good Chinese restaurant?*
famous ['feɪməs]	berühmt	*Do you want to be famous?*
interesting ['ɪntrəstɪŋ]	interessant	*Is your job interesting?*
football ['fʊtbɔːl]	Fußball	*My sister plays football.*
(to) **guess** [ges]	(er)raten	*What's that? – Guess!*

Magazine

(to) **eat** [iːt]	essen	*I eat a lot of Chinese food.*
radio ['reɪdɪəʊ]	Radio	*I listen to the radio in the morning.*
cards [kɑːdz]	Karten	
butter ['bʌtə]	Butter	
chocolate ['tʃɒklət]	Schokolade	
best [best]	beste/r/s	
thing [θɪŋ]	Sache, Ding, Gegenstand	*What's the best thing about your job?*
canteen [kæn'tiːn]	Kantine	*The actor is in the canteen.*
centre ['sentə]	Zentrum	*My sister lives in the centre of New York.*
holiday ['hɒlədeɪ]	Ferien, Urlaub	*Where do you go on holiday?*
(to) **speak** [spiːk]	sprechen	*Speak to me, please.*
(to) **speak to sb** ['spiːk tʊ]	mit jdm sprechen	*Can I speak to Mr Jones, please?*
in this photo [ɪn ðɪs 'fəʊtəʊ]	auf diesem Foto	*How many people are in this photo?*
(to) **be on holiday** [biː ən 'hɒlədeɪ]	im Urlaub sein	*My sister is on holiday.*
sure [ʃʊə]	sicher	*Are you sure?*
(to) **be sure** [biː 'ʃʊə]	sich sicher sein	*I'm sure she's a teacher.*
party [dɒg]	Party	
ideal [aɪ'diːəl]	ideal	*What's your ideal job?*
neighbour ['neɪbə]	Nachbar/in	*My ideal neighbours have children.*
lots of ['lɒts əv]	viel, viele	*Lots of people like gardening.*
dog [dɒg]	Hund	
garden ['gɑːdn]	Garten	*What a nice garden.*
like [laɪk]	wie	

! Chocolate lässt sich im Englischen sowohl essen als auch trinken.

TRANSCRIPT

TRANSCRIPT

(to) **look like** ['lʊk laɪk]	aussehen wie	*She looks like your mother.*
gardener ['gɑːdnə]	Gärtner/in	*My mother-in-law is a gardener.*
myself [maɪ'self]	selbst	*I like gardens. I'm a gardener myself.*
television ['telɪvɪʒn]	Fernsehen	*Hey, you're on television. Look.*
(to) **watch television** [wɒtʃ 'telɪvɪʒn]	fernsehen	*I don't watch much television.*
at night [ət 'naɪt]	nachts	*My neighbour sings late at night.*
(to) **get up** [ˌget 'ʌp]	aufstehen	*I get up early in the morning.*
every ['evri]	jede/r/s	*I get up late every weekend.*
(to) **invite** [ɪn'vaɪt]	einladen	
(to) **have a party** [həv ə 'pɑːti]	eine Party feiern	
of course [əf 'kɔːs]	natürlich, selbstverständlich	
always ['ɔːlweɪz]	immer	
for example [fər ɪg'zɑːmpl]	zum Beispiel	*I like music, Beethoven, for example.*
(to) **need to** ['niːd tə]	müssen	*I need to borrow a mobile phone.*
(to) **borrow** ['bɒrəʊ]	(sich etwas) ausleihen	
tool [tuːl]	Werkzeug	*Can I borrow some tools, please?*
litre (of sth) ['liːtər əv]	Liter	*Can I have litre of milk, please?*
milk [mɪlk]	Milch	*I like milk.*

! Have taucht in vielen Wendungen auf, in denen es nicht immer mit „haben" übersetzt wird. Bitte die Wendungen als solche lernen.

daughter-in-law ['dɔːtərɪnlɔː]	Schwiegertochter	**grandmother** ['grænmʌðə]	Großmutter
brother-in-law ['brʌðərɪnlɔː]	Schwager	**granddaughter** ['grændɔːtə]	Enkelin
nephew ['nevjuː]	Neffe	**uncle** ['ʌŋkl]	Onkel
niece [niːs]	Nichte	**cousin** ['kʌzn]	Cousin/e
mother-in-law ['mʌðərɪnlɔː]	Schwiegermutter	**aunt** [ɑːnt]	Tante
sister-in-law ['sɪstərɪnlɒː]	Schwägerin	**grandson** ['grænsʌn]	Enkel

under ['ʌndə]	unter	
wonderful [wʌndəfl]	wunderbar	*She's a wonderful baby.*

Story

still [stɪl]	(immer) noch	*Oh dear. So late and I'm still in the office.*
next [nekst]	nächste/r/s	*Who's next?*
(to) **come** [kʌm]	kommen	*Can I come with you?*
minute ['mɪnɪt]	Minute	*The next bus is in 20 minutes.*
(to) **explode** [ɪk'spləʊd]	explodieren	*Mrs Morgan explodes.*
(to) **get on (well) with sb** [ˌget ɒn 'wel wɪð]	(gut) mit jdm auskommen	*Winston and Ben get on well.*
difficult ['dɪfɪkəlt]	schwer, schwierig	*Mother-in-laws are always difficult.*
just [dʒʌst]	(ganz) einfach	*They just don't get on.*

That's life! — *So ist das Leben!*

UNIT 4

Focus 1

favourite ['feɪvərɪt]	liebste/r/s, Lieblings-	*I love pizza. It's my favourite food.*
world [wɜːld]	Welt	*It's a small world.*
from around the world [frəm əˌraʊnd ðə 'wɜːld]	aus der ganzen Welt	*I love music from around the world.*
quiz [kwɪz]	Quiz	*We always go to the pub quiz on Friday evening.*
(to) **compare** [kəm'peə]	vergleichen	*Compare the pictures, please.*
pair [peə]	Paar	*Work with another pair, please.*

cheese [tʃiːz]	Käse	**butter** ['bʌtə]	Butter
beer [bɪə]	Bier	**tomato** [tə'mɑːtəʊ]	Tomate
kiwi ['kiːwiː]	Kiwi	**tomato ketchup** [tə'mɑːtəʊ ˌketʃʌp]	Ketchup
curry ['kʌri]	Curry	**mineral water** ['mɪnərəl ˌwɔːtə]	Mineralwasser
sushi ['suːʃi]	*jap. Fischgericht*	**wine** [waɪn]	Wein
whisky ['wɪski]	Whisky	**dessert** [dɪ'zɜːt]	Nachspeise, Dessert
vodka ['vɒdkə]	Wodka	**banana** [bə'nɑːnə]	Banane

Eine Liste mit Ländernamen und Nationalitäten finden Sie auf Seite 76–77.

Focus 2

(to) **eat out** [ˌiːt 'aʊt]	im Restaurant essen	*Do you like eating out?*
(to) **hate** [heɪt]	hassen, gar nicht mögen	*I hate football.*
(to) **love** [lʌv]	lieben, gern mögen	*I love books.*
me too [ˌmiː 'tuː]	ich auch	*I like Guinness. – Me too.*
me neither [miː 'naɪðə]	ich auch nicht	*I don't like sushi. – Me neither.*
What about ... ? ['wɒt əbaʊt]	Was ist mit ... ?	*What about you? Do you like Chinese food?*
really ['rɪəli]	wirklich, tatsächlich	*Do you really like fast food?*
never ['nevə]	nie(mals)	*She never drinks vodka.*
(to) **try** [traɪ]	probieren	*Try this. It's good.*
I've never tried it.	Ich habe es nie probiert.	
quite [kwaɪt]	ziemlich	*Beer is too bitter for me. – Really? I quite like it.*
I quite like it.	Ich mag es ganz gern.	
(to) **prefer** [prɪ'fɜː]	lieber mögen, bevorzugen	*I don't like hamburgers. I prefer spaghetti.*
hungry ['hʌŋgri]	hungrig	*I am hungry!*
interview ['ɪntəvjuː]	Interview	*Paco has an interview with Ben.*
popular ['pɒpjələ]	beliebt, populär	*Football is very popular in England.*

fish [fɪʃ]	Fisch	*I don't like fish much.*
not at all [nɒt ət 'ɔ:l]	überhaupt nicht	*I don't like fish at all.*
meat [mi:t]	Fleisch	*Do you eat lots of meat?*
vegetarian [ˌvedʒə'teərɪən]	Vegetarier/in	*My son's a vegetarian. He doesn't eat meat.*
card [kɑ:d]	Visitenkarte	*Here's my card.*
town [taʊn]	Stadt	*The Taj Mahal is the best restaurant in town.*
large [lɑ:dʒ]	groß	*Russia is a large country.*
selection [sɪ'lekʃn]	Auswahl	*They have a great selection of food and wine.*
weekend [ˌwi:k'end]	Wochenende	*What do you do at the weekend?*
special [speʃl]	besondere/r/s, Spezial-	*I'd like the special menu of the day, please.*
as much as ['əz 'mʌtʃ əz]	so viel wie	*Speak English as much you can.*
buffet ['bʊfeɪ]	Büfett	*Oh, what a wonderful buffet.*
us [ʌs]	uns	*We're tired. Can you take us home?*
service ['sɜ:vɪs]	Bedienung, Service	*The service is good.*
expensive [ɪk'spensɪv]	teuer	*Paris is expensive.*
there is ['ðeˌrɪz]	es gibt	! There is live music. ~~It gives~~ live music.
live music [laɪv 'mju:zɪk]	Livemusik	
market ['mɑ:kɪt]	Markt	*There is a market on Bond Street.*
each other [ˌi:tʃ 'ʌðə]	einander, gegenseitig	*Interview each other.*
near [nɪə]	in der Nähe von, nahe	*There's a nice restaurant near here.*
fantastic [fæn'tæstɪk]	fantastisch	*The food is fantastic.*
note [nəʊt]	Notiz	
guide [gaɪd]	Führer, Ratgeber	*The guide says that this place is really good.*
example [ɪg'zɑ:mpl]	Beispiel	*Write an example sentence.*

TRANSCRIPT

waiter, waitress ['weɪtə], ['weɪtrɪs]	Kellner/in	*The waiter is not very friendly.*
ham [hæm]	Schinken	*Would you like a ham sandwich?*
roll [rəʊl]	Brötchen	*I'd like a ham and cheese roll, please.*
how much [haʊ 'mʌtʃ]	wie viel	*How much money do you have?*
just [dʒʌst]	nur	*Just a glass of water, please.*
bill [bɪl]	Rechnung	*Darling, is it o.k. if you pay the bill …?*
What would you like? [ˌwɒt wʊd ju 'laɪk]	Was hätten Sie gern?	*What would you like? – A glass of water, please.*
(to) **have sth to eat** [həv ˌsʌmθɪŋ tə 'iːt]	etwas essen	
(to) **take away** [ˌteɪk ə'weɪ]	mitnehmen	*Can I have a sandwich to take away?*
(to) **drink** [drɪŋk]	trinken	*Does he drink tea or coffee?*
medium ['miːdiəm]	mittel	*A medium capuccino, please.*
small [smɔːl]	klein	*I live in a small house.*
anything ['enɪθɪŋ]	etwas	*Hi Mum! Is there anything to eat?*
anything else? [ˌenɪθɪŋ 'els]	noch etwas?	*Would you like anything else?*
euro ['jʊərəʊ]	Euro	*$ 250. How much is that in euro?*
business trip ['bɪznəs trɪp]	Geschäftsreise	*Tara is on her way home from a business trip.*
(to) **drop** [drɒp]	fallen lassen	*Oh, I dropped my ticket.*
boarding card ['bɔːdɪŋ kɑːd]	Bordkarte	*Oh no, where's my boarding card?*
(to) **happen** ['hæpən]	passieren, geschehen	*What happened?*
ending ['endɪŋ]	Ende	*That story can't have a happy ending.*
plane [pleɪn]	Flugzeug	*We are on different planes.*

Magazine

customer ['kʌstəmə]	Kunde/Kundin	*The customer is always right.*
(to) **drive** [draɪv]	(Auto) fahren	*I drive my husband to work.*

fast ['fɑ:st]	schnell	*Do you like fast cars?*
car [kɑ:]	Auto	*I don't drive a car.*
attractive [ə'træktɪv]	attraktiv, anziehend	*He's an attractive man.*
chicken wings ['tʃɪkɪn wɪŋz]	Hähnchenflügel	*I'd like the chicken wings with chips, please.*
cookie ['kʊki]	Plätzchen, Keks	*Let's have a chocolate cookie.*
(to) **go out** [ˌgəʊ 'aʊt]	ausgehen	*I would like to go out this evening.*
(to) **enjoy** [ɪn'dʒɔɪ]	genießen	*I enjoy my life a lot.*
meal [mi:l]	Essen, Mahlzeit	*She likes English meals.*

(to) **go out for dinner**	im Restaurant zu Abend essen	**rice** [raɪs]	Reis
vegetable lasagne [ˌvedʒtəbl lə'zænjə]	Gemüse-Lasagne	**main course** [ˌmeɪn 'kɔ:s]	Hauptgericht
salad ['sæləd]	Salat	**chicken** ['tʃɪkɪn]	Huhn, Hähnchen
portion [pɔ:ʃn]	Portion	**fruit** [fru:t]	Obst, Früchte
chips [tʃɪps]	Pommes frites	**Good evening.**	Guten Abend.
table for two [ˌteɪbl fə 'tu:]	Tisch für zwei	**smoking** ['sməʊkɪŋ]	Raucher-
prawn cocktail [prɔ:n 'kɒkteɪl]	Krabbencocktail	**non-smoking** [ˌnɒn'sməʊkɪŋ]	Nichtraucher-
starter ['stɑ:tə]	Vorspeise	**over here** [ˌəʊvə 'hɪə]	hier drüben
baked camembert [beɪkt 'kæməmbeə]	gebackener Camembert	(to) **be ready to do sth** ['redi]	bereit sein, etwas zu tun
side dish ['saɪd dɪʃ]	Beilage	(to) **order** ['ɔ:də]	bestellen

Eating out

Would you like to have the menu?	Hätten Sie gerne die Speisekarte?
What would you like?	Was möchten Sie gerne essen/trinken?
I'd like …	Ich hätte/möchte gern …
Just a moment!	Einen Augenblick, bitte.
Would you like anything else?	Möchten Sie sonst noch etwas?
Just the bill, please.	Nur die Rechnung, bitte.
I'd like to pay now.	Ich würde jetzt gerne bezahlen.

film character ['fɪlm ˌkærəktə]	Filmfigur	*ET is a film character.*

Story

sales manager ['seɪlz ˌmænɪdʒə]	Verkaufsleiter/in	*The sales manager loves popcorn.*
travel firm ['trævl fɜːm]	Reiseveranstalter	*Paco is the sales manager of a travel firm.*
(to) **organize** ['ɔːgənaɪz]	organisieren	*Paco's firm organizes holidays in Spain.*
alternative [ɔːl'tɜːnətɪv]	alternativ	*She listens to alternative music.*
activity holiday [æk'tɪvəti ˌhɒlədeɪ]	Aktivurlaub	*My parents love activity holidays.*
northern ['nɔːðən]	Nord-, nördlich	*Northern Scotland isn't warm in December.*
goodbye [ˌgʊd'baɪ]	auf Wiedersehen	*Goodbye. Have a good holiday.*
(to) **say goodbye**	sich verabschieden	*Tara and Paco say goodbye.*
baggage hall ['bægɪdʒ hɔːl]	Gepäckhalle	*I have to wait in the baggage hall.*
(to) **collect sth/sb** [kə'lekt]	etwas/jdn abholen	*I collect my son from school every day.*
suitcase ['suːtkeɪs]	Koffer	*Tara collects her suitcase from the baggage hall.*
hand baggage ['hænd bægɪdʒ]	Handgepäck	*You can take hand baggage on the plane.*
straight through [streɪt 'θruː]	direkt durch	*Go straight through to the baggage hall.*

Enjoy your meal! — *Guten Appetit!*

Thanks, you too! — *Danke, dir auch!*

UNIT 5

Focus 1

typical ['tɪpɪkl]	typisch	*What is a typical English meal?*
daily ['deɪli]	täglich	*I learn English daily.*
normal ['nɔːml]	normal	*How many new words do you learn on a normal day?*
breakfast ['brekfəst]	Frühstück	*When do you eat breakfast?*

at home [ət 'həʊm]	zu Hause	*I eat at home on a normal weekday.*
main meal [meɪn 'mi:l]	Hauptmahlzeit	*When do you eat your main meal?*
a lot of [ə 'lɒt əv]	viel, viele	*A lot of people don't have lunch at work.*
group profile ['gru:p ˌprəʊfaɪl]	Gruppenprofil	*Do we have a group profile?*
(to) **interview** ['ɪntəvju:]	befragen, interviewen	*Ben interviews Paco about his company.*
habit ['hæbɪt]	Angewohnheit	*Tell me about your eating habits.*
(to) **take notes** [teɪk 'nəʊts]	sich Notizen machen	*Can you take notes, please?*
(to) **report sth to sb** [rɪ'pɔ:t]	jdm etwas berichten	
most [məʊst]	die meisten	! Most people like chocolate. ~~The most people like chocolate.~~
middle ['mɪdl]	Mitte	
middle of the day [ˌmɪdl əv ðə 'deɪ]	Mitte des Tages	*I'm always hungry in the middle of the day.*
for breakfast [fə 'brekfəst]	zum Frühstück	*I eat toast for breakfast.*
(to) **have/eat breakfast** [həv/i:t 'brekfəst]	frühstücken	*When do you have breakfast?*
lunch [lʌntʃ]	Mittagessen	*Lunch is from 12.00 to 14.00.*
(to) **have/eat lunch** [həv/i:t 'lʌntʃ]	zu Mittag essen	*Do you have lunch in the canteen?*
park [pɑ:k]	Park	*There are wonderful parks in Cardiff.*

Focus 2

routine [ru: 'ti:n]	Routine, Tagesablauf	*Talk about your daily routines.*
time [taɪm]	Uhrzeit	*What time is it?*
clock [klɒk]	Uhr	*Is there a clock in your office?*
o'clock [ə'klɒk]	(um) ... Uhr	*6.00 = It's six o'clock.*
a.m. (ante meridiem) [ˌeɪ 'em]	von Mitternacht bis Mittag	*The bus leaves at 6 a.m.*
p.m. (post meridiem) [ˌpi: 'em]	von Mittag bis Mitternacht	*Can we meet at ten? – Ten a.m. or p.m.?*
past [pɑ:st]	nach	*8.05 = It's five past eight.*

half past (six) [ˌhɑːf ˈpɑːst sɪks]	halb sieben	*8.30 = half past eight*
quarter past [ˈkwɔːtə pɑːst]	Viertel nach	*8.15 = quarter past eight*
quarter to [ˈkwɔːtə tu]	Viertel vor	*7.45 = quarter to eight*
between [bɪˈtwiːn]	zwischen	*I always have lunch between 12 and 1 p.m.*
afternoon [ˌɑːftəˈnuːn]	Nachmittag; Nachmittags-	*He sleeps in the afternoon.*
travel company [ˈtrævl ˌkʌmpəni]	Reiseunternehmen	
(to) **start** [stɑːt]	anfangen, beginnen	*I start work in the morning.*
(to) **go shopping** [ˌgəʊ ˈʃɒpɪŋ]	einkaufen gehen	*Many people go shopping on Saturday.*
quick [kwɪk]	schnell	*I have a quick snack before I go to work.*
cup [kʌp]	Tasse	*I had a cup of tea this morning.*
usually [ˈjuːʒuəli]	normalerweise, gewöhnlich	*He usually goes to his English class on Monday.*
at least [ət ˈliːst]	zumindest, mindestens	*Write at least three sentences.*
city [ˈsɪti]	(Groß)-Stadt	*Is it better to live in a small town or a city?*
(to) **finish** [ˈfɪnɪʃ]	beenden, aufhören	*When do you finish work?*
sometimes [ˈsʌmtaɪmz]	manchmal	*She sometimes drinks beer after work.*
glass [glɑːs]	Glas	*I'd like a glass of wine, please.*
old [əʊld]	alt	*How old are you? – 29.*
part [pɑːt]	Teil	*The ending is the best part of the film.*
him [hɪm]	ihn, ihm	*Can you give him a message?*
chat [tʃæt]	Unterhaltung, Gespräch	*We often have a chat with our teacher after class.*
bed [bed]	Bett	*I love my bed!*
(to) **go to bed** [gəʊ tə ˈbed]	ins Bett gehen	*And when do you go to bed?*
before [bɪˈfɔː]	vor	*I have breakfast before 8.00.*
midnight [ˈmɪdnaɪt]	Mitternacht	*Paco and his wife go to bed after midnight.*

why [waɪ]	warum	*Why are you so happy?*
long [lɒŋ]	lang	*Do you have a long way to work?*
working day ['wɜːkɪŋ deɪ]	Arbeitstag	*Paco has a long working day.*
where [weə]	wohin	*Where are you going?*
break [breɪk]	Pause	*I have a coffee break at 10.00.*
straight [streɪt]	direkt	*They go straight home.*
(to) **decide** [dɪ'saɪd]	entscheiden	*Why is it sometimes so difficult to decide?*

Focus 3

factory ['fæktəri]	Fabrik	*I live near a chocolate factory.*
worker ['wɜːkə]	Arbeiter/in	*Deng Bing Yu is a factory worker.*
hard [hɑːd]	schwer, hart	*She works ten hours a day. She works hard.*
(to) **sleep** [sliːp]	schlafen	*Most people sleep at night.*
back [bæk]	zurück	*She's back at school in the afternoon.*
till [tɪl]	bis	*On a weekday I sleep till 7 a.m.*
days a week [ˌdeɪzə'wiːk]	Tage in der Woche	*How many days a week do you work? – Four.*
Sunday ['sʌndeɪ]	Sonntag	*Most people don't work on Sunday.*
(to) **have to** ['həv tʊ]	müssen	*Li Yan has to work in her holidays.*
service job ['sɜːvɪs dʒɒb]	Dienstleistungsberuf	*A service job can be stressful.*
open ['əʊpən]	offen, geöffnet	*Shops are open till late in the evening.*
summer ['sʌmə]	Sommer	*Do English children have long summer holidays?*
winter ['wɪntə]	Winter	*I would like to have a winter holiday.*
(to) **teach** [tiːtʃ]	unterrichten	
homework ['həʊmwɜːk]	Hausaufgaben	
kilometre ['kɪləmiːtə]	Kilometer	

!
I have a lot of homework.
~~I have a lot of homeworks.~~

FILES

FILES

practical ['præktɪkl]	praktisch	*It's so practical to have a bike here.*
final ['faɪnl]	letzte/r/s	*It's Jang Wenwen's final year at school.*
on Sunday [ɒn 'sʌndeɪ].	sonntags	*I get up late on Sunday.*
from time to time [frəm ˌtaɪm tə 'taɪm]	von Zeit zu Zeit	*I go to a restaurant from time to time.*
schoolchild ['sku:ltʃaɪld]	Schulkind	*Schoolchildren work hard in China.*

Magazine

midday [ˌmɪd'deɪ]	Mittag, mittags	*We have lunch at midday.*
noon [nu:n]	Mittag	*Cowboys always meet at noon.*
studio ['stju:dɪəʊ]	Studio	*I'd like to work in a TV studio.*
(to) **get to the TV studio** [ˌget tə ðə ˌti: 'vi: ˌstju:diəʊ]	im Fernsehstudio ankommen	*The presenter gets to the TV studio at 4.30.*
(to) **get back home** [ˌget bæk 'həʊm]	wieder nach Hause kommen	*When do you normally get back home?*
T **TV presenter** [ti:'vi: prɪˌzentə]	Fernsehmoderator/in	! movie (AE) film (BE)
movie *(AE)* ['mu:vi]	Film	
Excuse me … [ɪk'skju:z mi]	Entschuldigung …	
shower ['ʃaʊə]	Dusche	*We have a nice big shower.*
(to) **shower** ['ʃaʊə]	(sich) duschen	*I shower every morning.*
(to) **have a shower** *(BE)* [həv ə 'ʃaʊə]	(sich) duschen	*After sport I have a shower.*
(to) **number** ['nʌmbə]	nummerieren	*Please number your sentences.*
action ['ækʃn]	Handlung; Aktion	*My first daily action is to make coffee.*
order ['ɔ:də]	Reihenfolge	*Please put the words in the right order.*
normally ['nɔ:məli]	normalerweise	*Who normally feeds the cat?*
cross [krɒs]	Kreuz	*Put a cross here.*
(to) **get dressed** [get 'drest]	(sich) anziehen	*They get dressed late on Sunday.*
(to) **switch on** [ˌswɪtʃ 'ɒn]	an-, einschalten	*Stop talking! Switch on the TV.*

coffee machine ['kɒfɪ məˌʃi:n]	Kaffeemaschine	*Can you switch on the coffee machine, please?*
(to) **take a shower** (*AE*) [ˌteik ə 'ʃauːə]	sich duschen	*He takes a cold shower in the morning.*
bathroom ['ba:θrʊm]	Bad	*Where's the bathroom, please?*
(to) **switch off** [ˌswɪtʃ 'ɒf]	ausschalten	*Oh, please switch off the alarm clock!*
alarm clock [ə'lɑ:m klɒk]	Wecker	
(to) **brush your teeth** (*BE*) [ˌbrʌʃ jə 'ti:θ]	sich die Zähne putzen	
(to) **feed** [fi:d]	füttern	
cat [kæt]	Katze	
(to) **go jogging** [gəʊ 'dʒɒgɪŋ]	Joggen	*On a typical day I go jogging at 6 a.m.*
newspaper ['nju:zpeɪpə]	Zeitung	*I often read the newspaper on the way to work.*
kitchen [kitʃɪn]	Küche	*We always eat in the kitchen.*
(to) **make coffee** [meɪk 'kɒfi:]	Kaffee kochen	*Please make coffee straight away.*
after that [ˌɑ:ftə 'ðæt]	danach	*I shower and after that I brush my teeth.*
(to) **go back** [gəʊ 'bæk]	zurückgehen	*I want to go back to bed.*

! Manches macht man in GB und den USA unterschiedlich:
AE: (to) take a shower
BE: (to) have a shower
BE: (to) brush your teeth
AE: (to) clean your teeth

TRANSCRIPT

Story

(to) **be interested in sth** [bi 'ɪntrəstɪd ɪn]	an etwas interessiert sein	*She is very interested in languages.*
green [gri:n]	grün	*Yuk. The cheese is green!*
tourism ['tʊərɪzəm]	Tourismus	*Is international tourism a good thing?*
green tourism ['gri:n ˌtʊərɪzəm]	alternativer Tourismus	*Ben's article is about green tourism.*
after ['ɑ:ftə]	nach	*Can we have a drink after class?*
article ['ɑ:tɪkl]	Artikel	*This journalist writes really good articles.*
(to) **be happy about sth** [bi 'hæpi]	über etwas erfreut/ glücklich sein	*I'm happy about my new job.*
too [tu:]	zu	*It's too late now.*

reader ['riːdə]	Leser/in	*Most of our online readers are German.*
that sort of topic [ðæt ˌsɔːt əv 'tɒpɪk]	solche/derlei Themen	*I'm interested in "green tourism" and that sort of topic.*
angry ['æŋgri]	verärgert, wütend	*Mrs Morgan was very angry with Ben.*

See you next week! — *Bis nächste Woche!*

Hope to see you, too. — *Ich hoffe auch, Sie/dich wieder zu sehen.*

UNIT 6

Focus 1

time expressions ['taɪm ɪkˌspreʃnz]	Zeitangaben	*Look at the time expressions, please.*
could [kʊd]	könnte/n	*I could visit you if you have time.*
definitely ['defɪnətli]	bestimmt, sicher(lich)	*Beer is definitely not my favourite drink.*
perhaps [pə'hæps]	vielleicht, eventuell	*Perhaps we can have a drink after work.*
it must be [ˌɪt 'mʌst ˌbi]	es muss … sein	*It must be almost time for lunch.*

Monday ['mʌndeɪ]	Montag	**Sunday** ['sʌndeɪ]	Sonntag
Tuesday ['tjuːzdeɪ]	Dienstag	**breakfast time** ['brekfəst taɪm]	Frühstückszeit
Wednesday ['wenzdeɪ]	Mittwoch	**lunchtime** ['lʌntʃtaɪm]	Mittagszeit, -pause
Thursday ['θɜːzdeɪ]	Donnerstag	**tea time** ['tiːtaɪm]	Teezeit
Friday ['fraɪdeɪ]	Freitag	**happy hour** ['hæpi aʊə]	Happy Hour
Saturday ['sætədeɪ]	Samstag	**dinner time** ['dɪnə taim]	(Abend-)Essenszeit

recording [rɪ'kɔ:dɪŋ]	Aufnahme, Aufzeichnung	*My album is ready for the recording studio.*
column ['kɒləm]	Spalte	*Sort the words into two columns.*
combination [ˌkɒmbɪ'neɪʃn]	Kombination, Verbindung	*Beer and wine is not a good combination.*
(to) **cook** [kʊk]	kochen	*Do you cook a meal in the evening?*
(to) **surf the internet** [sɜ:f ði: 'ɪntənet]	im Internet surfen	*How often do you surf the internet?*
brunch [brʌntʃ]	breakfast *und* lunch = Brunch	*Can we have brunch today?*
cake [keɪk]	Kuchen	*I like a piece of cake in the afternoon.*
CD [si:'di:]	CD	*That's a fantastic CD.*
church [tʃɜ:tʃ]	Kirche	*Do you sometimes go to church?*
cinema ['sɪnəmə]	Kino	*He often goes to the cinema.*
computer game [kəm'pju:tə geɪm]	Computerspiel	*Ben plays computer games in the evening.*
(to) **go dancing** [ˌgəʊ 'dɑ:nsɪŋ]	tanzen gehen	*They often go dancing on Saturdays.*
(to) **go swimming** [ˌgəʊ 'swɪmɪŋ]	schwimmen gehen	*I usually go swimming at the weekend.*
gym [dʒɪm]	Sportstudio, Fitnessstudio	*I don't often go to the gym.*
inline-skating ['ɪnlaɪnskeɪtɪŋ]	Inlineskaten	*Inline-skating in the house is not always a good idea.*
pub [pʌb]	Kneipe	*Would you like to go to the pub with me?*
sauna ['sɔ:nə]	Sauna	*I never go to the sauna at the weekend.*
video ['vɪdiəʊ]	Video(film)	*Let's watch a video.*
position [ˌpə'zɪʃn]	Stellung, Position	
once [wʌns]	einmal	
twice [twaɪs]	zweimal	
times [taɪmz]	mal	

Zeitangaben wie always, never, usw. stehen vor dem Hauptverb: I always get up early. Aber nach dem Verb (to) be: I'm never late.

–				+
never	**sometimes**	**often**	**usually**	**always**
nie(mals)	manchmal	oft	normalerweise	immer

tour [tʊə]	Tour, Reise	
postcard ['pəʊstkɑːd]	Postkarte	*He always writes nice postcards from Italy.*
stressed [strest]	betont	*Words like "a" are not usually stressed.*

Focus 2

TRANSCRIPT

leisure ['leʒə]	Freizeit	
activity [æk'tɪvəti]	Aktivität, Beschäftigung	
(to) **write down** ['wiːkli]	aufschreiben, notieren	*Don't you want to write that down?*
zoo [zuː]	Zoo	*Can we go to the zoo, mum?*
monkey ['mʌŋki]	Affe	*My brother is a little monkey.*
(to) **adopt** [ə'dɒpt]	adoptieren	*We would love to adopt a baby.*
tiger ['taɪgə]	Tiger	*My son would like to adopt a tiger.*
call [kɔːl]	Anruf, Telefongespräch	*There's a call for you, Ben.*
(Are) things OK at work?	Ist beruflich alles in Ordnung?	*You look tired. Are things OK at work?*
actually ['æktʃuəli]	eigentlich, tatsächlich	*I'm actually away from home quite a lot.*
true [truː]	richtig, wahr	*Is that true?*
I mean [aɪ 'miːn]	ich sag' mal; na ja	*What do you think? – Well, I mean, I don't know …*
(to) **be out all the time**	die ganze Zeit unterwegs sein	*Tara is out all the time.*
dance class ['dɑːns klɑːs]	Tanzunterricht	*I'd like to go to a modern dance class.*
(to) **suppose** [sə'pəʊz]	annehmen, vermuten	*Tara? – She's at work, I suppose.*
I suppose so. [aɪ sə'pəʊz səʊ]	Ich denke schon.	*Is Tara in her office? – I suppose so.*
(to) **work out** ['wɜːk ˌaʊt]	(hart) trainieren	*I work out at the gym.*
right [raɪt]	okay, in Ordnung	*Can you have a look at this? – Right.*
age [eɪdʒ]	Alter	*Peope of all ages learn English.*
age group ['eɪdʒ gruːp]	Altersgruppe	*Do you meet people of a different age group?*

bank holiday [ˌbæŋk ˈhɒlədeɪ]	Feiertag	*It always rains on a bank holiday.*
national [ˈnæʃnəl]	national	*Wine is a national drink in France.*
botanic garden [beˌtænɪk ˈgɑːdn]	botanischer Garten	*There's a wonderful botanic garden in Berlin.*
horse [hɔːs]	Pferd	*I'm so hungry I could eat a horse.*
cart [kɑːt]	Kutsche	*I hate this old car. A cart would be faster.*
ride [raɪd]	Fahrt	*Children love horse and cart rides.*
closing time [ˈkləʊzɪŋ taɪm]	Ende der Öffnungszeit	*What happens in the zoo after closing time?*
north [ˌnɔːθ]	Nord-, nördlich	
entrance [ˈentrəns]	Eingang, Einfahrt	*Where's the entrance?*
guided walk [gaɪdɪd ˈwɔːk]	geführte Wanderung	*Let's have a guided walk through the kitchen.*
west [west]	West-, westlich	*Düsseldorf is in west Germany.*
adult [ˈædʌlt]	Erwachsene/r	*You're 50 years old. Please behave like an adult.*
education [ˌedʒuˈkeɪʃn]	Erziehung, Bildung	*Is the education system in Germany good?*
adult education [ˌædʌlt edʒuˈkeɪʃn]	Erwachsenenbildung	*She wants to do a course at the adult education centre.*
county coucil [ˈkaʊnti kaʊnsl]	Bezirksverwaltung	*We got money for the project from the county council.*
mixed [mɪkst]	gemischt	*Summer in Berlin is always mixed.*
ability [əˈbɪləti]	Fähigkeit	*She has a great ability to teach.*
finger [ˈfɪŋgə]	Finger	*How many fingers can you see?*
painting [ˈpeɪntɪŋ]	Malen	*My wife likes painting.*
leaflet [ˈliːflət]	Faltblatt	*Can you give me that leaflet, please?*
(to) **focus on** [ˈfəʊkəs ɒn]	sich konzentrieren auf	*You need to focus on your English.*
indoor [ˈɪndɔː]	Innen-, Hallen-	*Indoor football is fun.*
outdoor [ˈaʊtdɔː]	im Freien	*You can do a lot of outdoor activities in summer.*
event [ɪˈvent]	Ereignis, Veranstaltung	*Carnival is always a happy event.*
all year round [ɔːl jɪə ˈraʊnd]	das ganze Jahr über	*She goes to the gym all year round.*

What kind of ... ?	Was für ein/e ... ?	*What kind of party?*
shall [ʃəl]	sollen; werden	*Where shall we go on holiday this year?*
(to) **take place** [teɪk 'pleɪs]	stattfinden	*The festival takes place in Brighton.*
(to) **need** [ni:d]	benötigen, brauchen	*I sometimes just need some chocolate.*
tour guide ['tʊə gaɪd]	Reisefüher/in	*I'd like to be a tour guide in Oxford.*
month [mʌnθ]	Monat	*Can we go to the theatre this month?*
building ['bɪldɪŋ]	Gebäude	*She went into the building.*
(to) **visit** ['vɪzɪt]	besuchen	*She visits her grandmother every Tuesday.*
meaning ['mi:nɪŋ]	Bedeutung, Sinn	*What's the meaning of life?*
(to) **highlight** ['haɪlaɪt]	hervorheben, unterstreichen	*I'd like to highlight some of the problems.*
(to) **pick up** [,pɪk 'ʌp]	abholen	*He picks up the children from school every day.*
tourist ['tʊərɪst]	Tourist/in	*Oh, he must be a tourist.*
city centre [,sɪti 'sentə]	Stadtzentrum	*Let's meet in the city centre.*
sights [saɪts]	Sehenswürdigkeiten	*Are there any sights to see in Hanover?*
castle ['kɑ:sl]	Burg, Schloss	*The Queen has lots of castles.*
visitor ['vɪzɪtə]	Besucher/in	*Who was your attractive visitor yesterday?*
(to) **taste** [teɪst]	*(Speisen)* probieren, versuchen	*I'll taste anything once.*
(to) **learn** [lɜ:n]	lernen	*Travelling is a good way to learn about life.*
language ['læŋgwɪdʒ]	Sprache	*How many languages do you speak?*

Magazine

(to) **smoke** [sməʊk]	rauchen	*She smokes in the bathroom.*
cook [kʊk]	Koch/Köchin	*My mum is the best cook in the world.*
midnight sun [,mɪdnaɪt 'sʌn]	Mitternachtssonne	
busy ['bɪzi]	beschäftigt	
boyfriend ['bɔɪfrend]	Freund	

T

! „Normale" Freunde und Freundinnen sind im Englischen friends. Boyfriends und girlfriends sind Partner.

(to) **sell** [sel]	verkaufen	*Do you sell things on the internet?*
idea [aɪ'dɪə]	Idee, Gedanke	*That's a good idea!*
category ['kætəgəri]	Kategorie	*Put the words into the correct category.*
brochure ['brəʊʃə]	Broschüre	*I need the brochure to plan my holiday.*
photography [fə'tɒgrəfɪ]	Fotografie	*I would like to do a course in photography.*
computing [kəm'pju:tɪŋ]	EDV	*Do you want to do a class in computing?*
beginner [bɪ'gɪnə]	Anfänger/in	*Computing for beginners.*
scuba-diving ['sku:bə daɪvɪŋ]	Sporttauchen *(mit Tauchgerät)*	*Scuba-diving around Mauritius is great.*
sailing ['seɪlɪŋ]	Segeln	*Do you go sailing in summer?*
modern ['mɒdn]	modern	*Do you think the Queen is a modern woman?*
modern dance [ˌmɒdn 'dɑ:ns]	moderner Tanz	*I like modern dance.*
cooking ['kʊkɪŋ]	Kochen	*Can you do the cooking today?*
landscape ['lændskeɪp]	Landschaft	*The landscape in Wales is beautiful.*
landscape gardening [ˌlændskeɪp 'gɑ:dnɪŋ]	Landschaftsgärtnerei	*My hobbies are painting and landscape gardening.*
creativity [ˌkri:eɪ'tɪvəti]	Kreativität	
practical ['præktɪkl]	praktisch	*Are you a practical sort of person?*
skill [skɪl]	Fähigkeit, Fertigkeit	*You need a lot of skills to be a good journalist.*
practical skills ['præktɪkl skɪlz]	praktische Fähigkeiten	*He doesn't have any practical skills.*
water sports ['wɒtə spɔ:ts]	Wassersport	*Are you interested in water sports?*
offer ['ɒfə]	Angebot	*Malta, Greece, Italy – what's the best offer?*
(to) **sail** ['seɪl]	segeln	*Can you sail?*
How about … ? ['haʊ əbaʊt]	Wie wär's mit … ?	*How about lunch? Are you hungry?*
(to) **dive** [daɪv]	tauchen	*I can only dive in a swimming pool.*
lake [leɪk]	See	*Are there any lakes in Berlin?*

TRANSCRIPT

ever ['evə]	jemals, überhaupt	*15 hours at work. – That was the longest day ever.*
maybe ['meɪbi]	vielleicht	*I would like to go to Malta or maybe Italy.*
creative [kri'eɪtɪv]	kreativ, schöpferisch	*She paints, she cooks. She's a very creative person.*
(to) **paint** [peɪnt]	malen	*Can you paint a picture of me?*
perfect ['pɜːfekt]	perfekt	*What's the perfect holiday for you?*
(to) **get** [get]	bekommen, erlangen	*I want to get some practical skills.*
at the same time [ət ðə ˌseɪm 'taɪm]	gleichzeitig	*I'm tired but happy at the same time.*
excellent ['eksələnt]	ausgezeichnet, hervorragend	*Thank you for an excellent meal.*
secret ['siːkrɪt]	Geheimnis	*Learn the secrets of cooking.*
lots of [lɒts əf]	viele, eine Menge	*There are lots of things you can do in London.*
fresh [frəʃ]	frisch	*I love fresh air.*
air [eə]	Luft	*I need some fresh air.*

Story

romantic [rəʊ'mæntɪk]	romantisch	*What a romantic story!*
window ['wɪndəʊ]	Fenster	*Can we have a table by the window?*
talk [tɔːk]	Gespräch, Unterhaltung	*They have a long talk about their problems.*
(to) **go away** [ˌgəʊ ə'weɪ]	wegfahren	*We want to go away, on holiday.*
everything ['evriθɪŋ]	alles	*Everything is planned.*
(to) **plan** [plæn]	planen	*Tara and Steve plan to go away.*
network ['netwɜːk]	Netz(werk)	*She has a network of friends.*

Cheers! [tʃɪəz] — *Prost!*

UNIT 7

Focus 1

yesterday ['jestədeɪ]	gestern	*What did you do yesterday?*
(to) **get about** [ˌget ə'baʊt]	herumkommen, sich fortbewegen	*How do you usually get about town?*
(to) **take** [teɪk]	nehmen	*Can you take me to town tomorrow?*
cow [kaʊ]	Kuh	*How's the cow? – Much better, thanks.*
editor ['edɪtə]	Redakteur/in	*She's an editor for the local newspaper.*
passenger ['pæsɪndʒə]	Passagier	*There are so many passengers on the morning trains.*
train [treɪn]	Zug	*I love old trains.*
own [əʊn]	eigene/r/s	*Serena has her own business.*
career [kə'rɪə]	Karriere	*She started her career as the editor of a magazine.*
wheel [wi:l]	Rad	*My car only has three wheels.*
ago [ə'gəʊ]	vor	*Two days ago I cooked a meal for friends.*
there are [ðeə 'rɑ:]	es gibt	*There are a lot of lakes in Berlin.*
already [ɔ:'ledɪ]	schon	*Is it already six o'clock?*
(to) **get somewhere** ['get ˌsʌmweə]	irgendwo hinkommen	*What time do you usually get home?*

(to) **get to work** [get tə 'wɜ:k]	zur Arbeit kommen	**by car** [baɪ 'kɑ:]	mit dem Auto
by bike [baɪ 'baɪk]	mit dem Rad	**by taxi** [baɪ 'tæksi]	mit dem Taxi
by train [baɪ 'treɪn]	mit der Bahn	**by underground** [baɪ 'ʌndəgraʊnd]	mit der U-Bahn
by bus [baɪ 'bʌs]	mit dem Bus		

rest [rest]	Ruhepause	*I think my teacher needs a rest.*
(to) **have a rest** [həv ə 'rest]	sich ausruhen	*I want to have a rest too.*
news [nju:z]	Nachrichten	*She listened to the news in the morning.*

guess [ges]	Vermutung	*Good guess! But wrong.*

Focus 2

regular [regjələ]	regelmäßig	*I am a regular visitor at the local cinema.*
irregular [ɪ'regjələ]	unregelmäßig	*Why are there so many irregular verbs in English?*
went [went]	*Vergangenheitsform von* go	*I went to a fantastic restaurant yesterday.*
had [hæd]	*Vergangenheitsform von* have	*We had a big dog when we were children.*
science ['saɪəns]	Wissenschaft	
politics ['pɒlətɪks]	Politik	*Don't start talking about politics again.*
money ['mʌni]	Geld	*He had no money left.*
(to) **spend money, spent** [spend 'mʌni], [spent]	Geld ausgeben	*I spent a lot of money on my last holiday.*
nothing ['nʌθɪŋ]	nichts	*There's nothing I can do for you.*
left [left]	übrig	*I'm sorry, there's nothing left to eat.*
got [gɒt]	*Vergangenheitsform von* get	*I got socks for Christmas this year.*
no [nəʊ]	kein/e	*I have no time for house-work.*
(to) **stay** [steɪ]	bleiben, wohnen	*Where do you usually stay on holiday?*
(to) **clean** [kli:n]	putzen, reinigen	*He always cleans the house at the weekend.*
(to) **save** [seɪv]	sparen	*We bought a robot to save time.*
enough [ɪ'nʌf]	ausreichend, genug	*I don't get enough sleep.*
bought [bɔ:t]	*Vergangenheitsform von* buy	*I bought so many nice things for my children.*
(to) **sort** [sɔ:t]	sortieren	*Let's sort our questions into the correct order.*
a long time ago [ə ˌlɒŋ taɪm ə'gəʊ]	vor langer Zeit	*I learned English a long time ago.*
last [lɑ:st]	zuletzt, das letzte Mal	*I last saw a movie two weeks ago.*
(to) **fly, flew** [flaɪ, flu:]	fliegen	*Last year I flew to Mauritius.*
flower ['flaʊə]	Blume	*Thank you for the beautiful flowers.*

somewhere ['sʌmweə]	irgendwohin	*When did you last fly somewhere?*
date [deɪt]	Verabredung	*You have a date? Who is it?*
(to) **have a date** [həv ə 'deɪt]	*(privat)* mit jdm verabredet sein	*Last Saturday Ben had a date with Sana.*
match [mætʃ]	Spiel, Match	*Come on. Let's go and see the match.*
(to) **lose, lost** [lu:z, lɒst]	verlieren	*I lost my keys yesterday.*
(to) **go for a drink** [ˌgəʊ fər ə 'drɪŋk]	einen trinken gehen	*Shall we go for a drink later?*
for long [fə 'lɒŋ]	lange	*Were you at home for long?*
(to) **come out of, came** [ˌkʌm 'aʊtəf]	herauskommen	*Ben came out of the pub.*
bus stop ['bʌs stɒp]	Bushaltestelle	*She walked to the bus stop.*
(to) **ring, rang** [rɪŋ], [ræŋ]	klingeln	*The phone rang.*
thought [θɔ:t]	*Vergangenheitsform von* think	*I thought a lot about you yesterday.*
(to) **want** [wɒnt]	wollen	*Is there anything you want from the bar?*
possible ['pɒsəbl]	möglich, denkbar	*Is Wednesday possible? Can we meet then?*
(to) **agree** [ə'gri:]	vereinbaren	*They agreed to see each other on Monday.*
piece [pi:s]	Stück	*Could you give me that piece of paper, please?*
(to) **run, ran** [rʌn], [ræn]	rennen, laufen	*He ran to meet her.*
underground ['ʌndəgraʊnd]	U-Bahn	*Sometimes it's very hot on the underground.*
station ['steɪʃn]	Bahnhof	*This morning I took a taxi to the station.*
closed [kləʊzd]	geschlossen, gesperrt	*The station was closed, so he took a taxi.*
lift [lɪft]	Aufzug, Fahrstuhl	*Can we please take the lift?*
(to) **be out of order** [bi: aʊt əv 'ɔ:də]	außer Betrieb sein	*The lift was out of order.*
took [tʊk]	*Vergangenheitsform von* take	*They took the train from Bristol to Cardiff.*
slow [sləʊ]	langsam	*The bus was very slow.*
(to) **be full of sth** [bi 'fʊl əv]	voller … sein	*The underground was full of people.*

traffic ['træfɪk]	(Straßen-)Verkehr	*Sorry I'm late. There was a lot of traffic.*
traffic lights ['træfɪk laɪts]	Ampel	*The traffic lights were red.*
red [red]	rot	*Watch out! The traffic lights are red!*
suddenly ['sʌdənli]	plötzlich	*Suddenly he saw his ex-wife.*
found [faʊnd]	*Vergangenheitsform von* find	*He found his sunglasses under the bed.*
jacket ['dʒækɪt]	Jacke, Jackett	*He found £20 in his jacket.*
(to) **stop (at)** [stɒp]	halten (an)	*The taxi stopped at the restaurant at 8.20.*
woman, women ['wʊmən, 'wɪmɪn]	Frau, Frauen	*Who's that woman in the photo?*
saw [sɔː]	*Vergangenheitsform von* see	*I saw our English teacher on Saturday.*
were [wɜː]	*Vergangenheitsform von* be	*Where were you?*

Magazine

village ['vɪlɪdʒ]	Dorf	*Do you live in a small village or a big town?*
young [jʌŋ]	jung	*She's a young career woman.*
(to) **have a good time** [həv ə gʊd 'taɪm]	sich amüsieren, viel Spaß haben	*We had a good time at the party.*
for the first time [fə ðə fɜːst 'taɪm]	zum ersten Mal	*When did you see him for the first time?*
Who did you go out with?	Mit wem warst du weg?	
drank [dræŋk]	*Vergangenheitsform von* drink	*Tara drank too much last night.*
transport [ˌtrænspɔːt]	öffentliche Verkehrsmittel; Transport	*How many transport words do you know in English?*
fact [fækt]	Tatsache, Fakt	
topic ['tɒpɪk]	Thema	*There's a lot to say about the topic of travelling.*
dictionary ['dɪkʃənri]	Wörterbuch	*Check new words in your dictionary.*
history ['hɪstri]	Geschichte	*The building has a very interesting history.*
BC [ˌbiː'siː]	*Abkürzung von* before Christ, vor Christus	
mile [maɪl]	Meile	*Oh dear! This is miles from home!*

platform ['plætfɔːm]	Gleis, Bahnsteig	**bus lane** ['bʌs leɪn]	Busspur
check-in desk ['tʃekɪn desk]	Abfertigungsschalter	**carriage** ['kærɪdʒ]	Wagen *(eines Zuges)*
cabin ['kæbɪn]	Kabine	**waiting room** ['weɪtɪŋ ˌruːm]	Warteraum
pilot ['paɪlət]	Pilot/in	**rickshaw** ['rɪkʃɔː]	Rikscha
railway ['reɪlweɪ]	Bahn, Eisenbahn	**cycle rickshaw** ['saɪkl ˌrɪkʃɔː]	Fahrradrikscha
gate ['geɪt]	Flugsteig	**camel** ['kæml]	Kamel
departure lounge [dɪ'pɑːtʃə laʊndʒ]	Abflughalle; Warteraum	**ski** [skiː]	Ski
bus shelter ['bʌs ˌʃeltə]	Bushäuschen	**tuk tuk** [tʊk tʊk]	motorisierte Rikscha
double-decker [ˌdʌbl'dekə]	Doppeldeckerbus	(to) **ride** [raɪd]	Fahrrad, Rikscha *oder* Motorrad fahren
duty-free shop [ˌduːtɪ'friːˌʃɒp]	Duty-free-Shop		

Story

conflict ['kɒnflɪkt]	Konflikt	*There is a lot of conflict in the world.*
(to) **escalate** ['eskəleɪt]	eskalieren	*Last week the conflict escalated.*
memo ['meməʊ]	Notiz, Vermerk	*Can you write me a memo?*
just [dʒʌst]	lediglich	*I just want on last chocolate.*
said [sed]	*Vergangenheitsform von* say	*She said she loved me.*
through [θruː]	durch	*She came in through the window.*
door [dɔː]	Tür	*The door was closed.*
(to) **sit down** [ˌsɪt 'daun]	sich setzen	*Sit down, please.*
(to) **give back, gave** [ˌgɪv 'bæk, geɪv]	zurückgeben	*Mrs Morgan gave him three articles back.*
knew [njuː]	*Vergangenheitsform von* know	*He knew she didn't like him.*
(to) **move** [muːv]	umziehen	*When I was a child, we often moved.*
downstairs [ˌdaʊn'steəz]	(nach) unten	*Let's go downstairs to the bathroom.*

basement ['beɪsmənt]	Untergeschoss	*My grandfather has some good wine in the basement.*
tomorrow [tə'mɒrəʊ]	morgen	*See you tomorrow.*

Have a great time!

Viel Spaß!

Thanks, same to you!

Danke gleichfalls!

UNIT 8

January ['dʒænjuəri]	Januar	**July** [dʒu'laɪ]	Juli
February ['februəri]	Februar	**August** ['ɔːgəst]	August
March [mɑːtʃ]	März	**September** [sep'tembə]	September
April ['eɪprəl]	April	**October** [ɒk'təʊbə]	Oktober
May [meɪ]	Mai	**November** [nəʊ'vembə]	November
June [dʒuːn]	Juni	**December** [dɪ'sembə]	Dezember

Focus 1

festival ['festɪvl]	Festival, Fest(spiele)	*a jazz festival*
century ['sentʃəri]	Jahrhundert	*In which century was Gandhi born?*
tradition [trə'dɪʃn]	Brauch, Tradition	*Do you have any special traditions in your family?*
(to) **steal, stole** [stiːl], [stəʊl]	stehlen	*Someone stole my bike last year.*
(to) **carry** ['kæri]	tragen	*I'll carry this box for you.*
(to) **take part in** [teɪk 'pɑːt ɪn]	teilnehmen an	*I'd like to take part in the Berlin marathon.*
championship ['tʃæmpɪənʃɪp]	Meisterschaft	*My favourite team won the championship!*
(to) **weigh** [weɪ]	wiegen	*How much did you weigh after Christmas?*

traditional [trə'dɪʃnl]	traditionell	
calendar ['kælɪndə]	Kalender	
thousands of … ['θaʊzndz əv]	Tausende …	*Thousands of people came to the concert.*
fireworks ['faɪəwɜːks]	Feuerwerk	
(to) **throw, threw** [θrəʊ], [θruː]	werfen	*Please, don't throw fireworks.*
Just for fun! [ˌdʒʌst fə 'fʌn]	Nur zum Spaß!	*Why did you do that? – Oh, just for fun.*
everyone ['evriwʌn]	jede/r/s	*Is everyone here today?*
man, men [mæn], [men]	Mann, Männer	*Do you know that man there?*
battle ['bætl]	Kampf, Schlacht	*Many men were lost in the battle.*
important [ɪm'pɔːtnt]	wichtig	*That's a very important question.*
illegal [ɪ'liːgl]	rechtswidrig, illegal	*It's illegal to work if you're under 14.*
legal ['liːgl]	rechtmäßig, legal	*She's the legal owner of the café.*
celebration [ˌselɪ'breɪʃn]	Feier	*We always have a big celebration at New Year.*
all over (the country) [ɔːl ˌəʊvə ðə 'kʌntri]	überall (im Land)	*People all over the country celebrated that night.*
wild [waɪld]	wild	*It was really wild!*
quiet ['kwaɪət]	ruhig	*It was a quiet day in the office, today.*

first [fɜːst]	erste/r/s	**ninth** [naɪnθ]	neunte/r/s
second ['sekənd]	zweite/r/s	**tenth** [tenθ]	zehnte/r/s
third [θɜːd]	dritte/r/s	**eleventh** [ɪ'levnθ]	elfte/r/s
fourth [fɔːθ]	vierte/r/s	**twelfth** [twelvθ]	zwölfte/r/s
fifth [fɪfθ]	fünfte/r/s	**thirteenth** [ˌθɜː'tiːnθ]	dreizehnte/r/s
sixth [sɪksθ]	sechst/r/s	**fourteenth** [ˌfɔː'tiːnθ]	vierzehnte/r/s
seventh ['sevnθ]	siebente/r/s	**fifteenth** [ˌfɪf'tiːnθ]	fünfzehnte/r/s
eighth [eɪtθ]	achte/r/s	**twenty-first** [ˌtwenti'fɜːst]	einundzwanzigste/r/s

date [deɪt]	Datum	*What's the date today?*
(to) **stand, stood** [stænd], [stʊd]	stehen	*We stood there and waited for the bus.*
(in) line [ɪn 'laɪn]	(in der) Reihe	*Is it really a British tradition to stand in line?*
according to [ə'kɔːdɪŋ tə]	gemäß, nach	
side [saɪd]	Seite	
When is your birthday?	Wann haben Sie / hast du Geburtstag?	
It's my birthday on …	Ich habe am … Geburtstag.	
What month is your birthday?	In welchem Monat haben Sie / hast du Geburtstag?	
What date is your birthday?	An welchem Datum haben Sie / hast du Geburtstag?	
nobody ['nəʊbədi]	niemand	
sick *(AE)* [sɪk]	krank	! sick (AE) ill (BE)
better ['betə]	besser	*I was ill last week, but I'm better now.*
I'm afraid … [aɪm ə'freɪd]	leider	*I'm afraid we're closed today.*
private ['praɪvət]	privat	*We have a private party.*
(to) **come in** [kʌm 'ɪn]	vorbeischauen	*You didn't come in last week.*
lovely ['lʌvli]	schön, herrlich	*You look lovely!*
voice [vɔɪs]	Stimme	*She has such a lovely voice.*
zero ['zɪərəʊ]	Null	

TRANSCRIPT

What can you say when somebody is ill

What's the matter?	Was ist los (mit Ihnen/dir)?
Oh dear! I'm sorry.	Oje! Das tut mir Leid.
I'm much better now, thanks.	Danke, mir geht's jetzt (wieder) viel besser.
I'm all right.	Mir geht es gut.
I'm not very well.	Ich fühle mich nicht sehr gut.
I'm sorry to hear that you're ill.	Es tut mir Leid zu hören, dass Sie krank sind/du krank bist.
I'm OK again.	Mir geht es wieder gut.

TRANSCRIPT

over there [ˌəʊvə 'ðeə]	da/dort (drüben)	*Is that Steve over there?*
system ['sɪstəm]	System	*I hate this computer system!*
athletic [æθ'letɪk]	sportlich	*She's very athletic. She runs to school every day.*
good wishes [gʊd 'wɪʃɪz]	Glückwünsche	

Good wishes

Happy New Year!	Glückliches Neues Jahr!
Thanks, and to you.	Danke gleichfalls.
Merry Christmas!	Frohe Weihnachten!
Thanks, and the same to you.	Danke gleichfalls.
Best wishes!	Alles Gute!
Good luck!	Viel Glück!

Focus 2

place [pleɪs]	Stelle, Platz, Ort	**winter holiday** ['wɪntə ˌhɒlədeɪ]	Winterurlaub
(to) **go on holiday** [gəʊ ɒn 'hɒlədeɪ]	in den Urlaub fahren	**package holiday** ['pækɪdʒ ˌhɒlədeɪ]	Pauschalreise
sea [siː]	Meer	**skiing** ['skiːɪŋ]	Skilaufen
by the sea [ˌbaɪ ðə 'siː]	am Meer, an der See	**souvenir** [ˌsuːvə'nɪə]	Andenken, Souvenir
mountain ['maʊntən]	Berg	**countryside** ['kʌntrisaɪd]	Landschaft
sun [sʌn]	Sonne	**cross-country** [ˌkrɒs 'kʌntri]	Langlauf-
flat *(BE)* [flæt]	Wohnung	**barbecue** ['bɑːbɪkjuː]	Grillparty
caravan ['kærəvæn]	Wohnwagen	(to) **lie, lay** [lai], [leɪ]	liegen
camping ['kæmpɪŋ]	Zelten, Camping	**beach** [biːtʃ]	Strand
wilderness ['wɪldənəs]	Wildnis		

(to) **go sightseeing** [gəʊ 'saɪtsiːɪŋ]	Sehenswürdigkeiten besuchen	*We went sightseeing last summer.*
(to) **go walking** [gəʊ 'wɔːkɪŋ]	wandern	*They go walking every Sunday.*

(to) **have a barbecue** [ˌhəv ə 'bɑːbɪkjuː]	grillen	*We often have barbecues in summer.*
(to) **lie on the beach** [ˌlaɪ ɒn ðə 'biːtʃ]	am Strand liegen	*On our last holiday we just lay on the beach.*
(to) **relax** [rɪ'læks]	(sich) entspannen	*I usually relax at the weekend.*
(to) **do nothing** [ˌduː 'nʌθɪŋ]	nichts tun	*On holiday I want to relax and do nothing.*
(to) **sit, sat** [sɪt], [sæt]	sitzen	*I like sitting in cafés.*
relative ['relətɪv]	Verwandte/r	*We visit relatives at Christmas.*
description [dɪ'skrɪpʃn]	Beschreibung	*That's a good description of the place.*
relaxing [rɪ'læksɪŋ]	erholsam, entspannend	*I love to have a relaxing bath after work.*
weather ['weðə]	Wetter	*The weather was bad.*
(to) **rain** [reɪn]	regnen	*It rained every day of our holidays.*
luxury ['lʌkʃəri]	Luxus	
timeline ['taɪmlaɪn]	Zeitachse	*Make your own personal learning timeline.*
(to) **pack** [pæk]	einpacken	*Remember to pack all the things you need.*
(to) **unpack** [ʌn'pæk]	auspacken	*When we unpacked our bag we found it wasn't ours.*
(to) **have a lie-in** [ˌhəv ə 'laɪ ɪn]	ausschlafen	*It's a luxury to have a lie-in at the weekend.*
(to) **retell** [ˌriː'tel]	nacherzählen	*I will retell the story to my grandchildren.*
heading ['hedɪŋ]	Überschrift	*Can you find a good heading for the text?*
destination [ˌdestɪ'neɪʃn]	Reise-, Fahrtziel	*What is your favorite holiday destination?*
accommodation [əˌkɒmə'deɪʃn]	Unterkunft	*Can you please find out about accomodation in Berlin?*
hot [hɒt]	heiß	*It's usually hot in the Sahara.*
bag [bæg]	Tasche	*What's in your bag?*
(to) **be missing** [bi 'mɪsɪŋ]	fehlen, verschwunden sein	*My bag was missing.*
(to) **discuss** [dɪ'skʌs]	besprechen, diskutieren	*We discussed the problem.*

Magazine

wall [wɔːl]	Wand, Mauer	
New Year's Eve [ˌnjuː jɪəz ˈiːv]	Silvester	
canal trip [kəˈnæl trɪp]	Kanalfahrt	
alone [əˈləʊn]	allein(e)	*Do you sometimes go on holiday alone?*
tent [tent]	Zelt	*We stayed in a tent on the beach.*
apartment *(AE)* [əˈpɑːtmənt]	Wohnung	*Do you live in your own house or apartment?*
place [pleɪs]	Ort	*We stayed in a really nice place in the mountains.*
stay [steɪ]	Aufenthalt	*We enjoyed our stay in Austria.*
daytime [ˈdeɪtaɪm]	tagsüber	*Some animals sleep daytime.*
(to) **end** [end]	enden	*How does the story end?*
surprise [səˈpraɪz]	Überraschung	*What a surprise to see you.*
visit [ˈvɪzɪt]	Besuch	*His visit was a nice surprise.*
supermarket [ˈsuːpəmɑːkɪt]	Supermarkt	*I don't go to the supermarket on Saturdays.*
navigation system [nævɪˈgeɪʃn ˌsɪstəm]	Navigationssystem	*Does your car have a navigation system?*
store *(AE)* [stɔː]	Geschäft, Warenhaus	*That's my favourite store.*
only [ˈəʊnli]	erst	*My son is only ten but he can speak English.*
(to) **come to a stop** [ˌkʌm tu ə ˈstɒp]	zum Halten kommen	*The bus came to a stop near my house.*
war [wɔː]	Krieg	
war veteran [wɔː ˈvetərən]	Kriegsveteran	
(to) **crash** [kræʃ]	aufprallen, zusammenstoßen	
police [pəˈliːs]	Polizei	
automatic [ˌɔːtəˈmætɪk]	automatisch	
box [bɒks]	Schachtel	*I ate a box of chocolates yesterday.*

(!) Achtung: Im Englischen fiel die Mauer nicht, sie kam herunter. The Berlin wall came down in 1989.

(!) Police ist immer Plural im Englischen: The police are here.

TRANSCRIPT

(to) **take sb to …** ['teɪk ˌsʌmbədi tə]	jdn mitnehmen, irgendwohin bringen	*The police took him to the police station.*
police station [pə'liːs steɪʃn]	Polizeiwache, -revier	
will [wɪl]	werden	*The words in the box will help you.*
cliff [klɪf]	Klippe, Felsen	*We went for a walk along the cliffs.*
(to) **build, built** [bɪld], [bɪlt]	bauen	*They built their own home.*
sandcastle ['sændkɑːsl]	Sandburg	
(to) **sunbathe** ['sʌnbeɪð]	sonnenbaden	*Where is the best place to sunbathe?*
back [bæk]	Rücken	*My father has a bad back.*
lobster ['lɒbstə]	Hummer	
sunny ['sʌni]	sonnig	*It's a sunny day.*
(to) **go for walks** [ˌgəʊ fə 'wɔːks]	spazieren gehen, wandern	*We went for a walk on the beach.*
dear [dɪə]	liebe/r	*"Dear Sarah. Thank you for your letter …"*
along [ə'lɒŋ]	entlang	*We walked along the cliffs to the hotel.*
(to) **get, got** [get], [gɒt]	werden	*After a day at the beach I get really hungry.*
wet [wet]	nass, feucht	*It rained a lot. Now it's wet outside.*
(to) **wish** [wɪʃ]	wünschen	*Wish you were here.*
Love, … [lʌv]	Alles Liebe, … *Briefschluss*	*See you soon. Love, Lucy.*

Story

argument ['ɑːgjumənt]	Auseinandersetzung, Streit	*Ben often has arguments with his boss.*
(to) **make printouts** ['meɪk ˌprɪntaʊts]	ausdrucken	
cardboard box ['kɑːdbɔːd bɒks]	Pappkarton	*I packed all my things into cardboard boxes.*
(to) **march** [mɑːtʃ]	marschieren	*He marched into the office.*
desk [desk]	Schreibtisch	*I have a mountain of paper on my desk.*
left [left]	*Vergangenheitsform von* leave	*He left the office.*

one more time [ˌwʌn mɔː ˈtaɪm]	noch einmal	*Play it one more time, please.*
without [wɪˈðaʊt]	ohne	*I'm without a car for the weekend.*
plan [plæn]	Plan	*He has many plans for the weekend.*

Have a good trip! — *Gute Reise!*

Thanks. I'm sure I will. — *Danke. Die werde ich sicherlich haben.*

Quick Check 2

(to) **bet** [bet]	wetten	*I bet my boyfriend can't carry me.*
You bet!	Und ob!	
Olympics [əˈlɪmpɪks]	Olympische Spiele	*Did you watch the Olympics on TV?*
(to) **laze about** [leɪz əˈbaʊt]	herumfaulenzen	*On Sundays I just laze about all day.*
awful [ˈɔːfl]	furchtbar, fürchterlich	*Oh no, it's that awful man again.*
sunshine [ˈsʌnʃaɪn]	Sonnenschein	*We had a lot of sunshine at the weekend.*

UNIT 9

Focus 1

ice cream parlour [ˈaɪs kriːm ˌpɑːlə]	Eisdiele	*It would be nice to work in an ice cream parlour.*
temple [ˈtempl]	Tempel	*There's a temple next door.*
town hall [ˌtaʊn ˈhɔːl]	Rathaus	*Many tourists come to visit our old town hall.*
chapel [ˈtʃæpl]	Kapelle	*My parents got married in a beautiful chapel.*
pond [pɒnd]	Teich	*My brother threw me in the pond when I was six.*
seat [siːt]	Sitz	*Please, take a seat.*

FILES Student A

inside [ɪn'saɪd]	innen, Innen(-)	*Let's go inside.*
boat [bəʊt]	Boot, Schiff	*Many people live on boats in summer.*
outside ['aʊtsaɪd]	außen, Außen(-)	*Brrh, it's cold outside.*
ceremony ['serəməni]	Zeremonie	*We saw a traditional ceremony in Thailand.*

FILES Student B

poor [pʊə]	arm	*There are many poor people in Latin America.*
however [haʊ'evə]	doch, jedoch	*Germany is rich. However, the people don't feel like it.*
rich [rɪtʃ]	reich, wohlhabend	
silver ['sɪlvə]	Silber	*He drives around town in a silver car.*

FILES Student C

(to) **serve** [sɜːv]	bedienen	*Why doesn't anybody come and serve us?*
roller skates ['rəʊlə ˌskeɪts]	Rollschuhe	*My boss often wears roller skates.*
Thai boxing ['taɪ bɒksɪŋ]	Thaiboxen	*She goes to a Thai boxing club on Mondays.*

FILES Student D

choice [tʃɔɪs]	Auswahl	*I can't decide, there's so much choice.*
flavour ['fleɪvə]	Geschmack, Aroma	*There are so many different flavours.*
vanilla [və'nɪlə]	Vanille	*I love apple pie with vanilla sauce.*
bean [biːn]	Bohne	*Do you like bean soup?*
tuna ['tjuːnə]	Tunfisch	*I'd like a tuna salad, please.*
rose [rəʊz]	Rose	*She gave me a rose!*

FILES Student E

floor [flɔː]	Fußboden	*The floor is so clean you could eat from it.*
art gallery ['ɑːt gæləri]	Kunstgalerie	*There's a new art gallery round the corner.*
temperature ['temprətʃə]	Temperatur	*In a perfect world the temperature would always be 25°.*
(to) **melt** [melt]	schmelzen	

Eine Liste mit Ländernamen und Nationalitäten finden Sie auf Seite 76–77.

comparison [kəm'pærɪsn]	Vergleich	*Germany is a very hot country in comparison to Siberia.*
high [haɪ]	hoch	*How high is Mount Everest? – 8,848 m.*

than [ðən]	als	*June is usually hotter than January.*
cold [kəʊld]	kalt	*Would you like a cold drink?*
warm [wɔːm]	warm	*I'm dreaming of a nice warm bed.*
worse [wɜːs]	*Komparativ von* bad, schlechter	*What is worse: no money, or no time?*
cheap [tʃiːp]	billig, günstig	*I got a cheap flight. It was only 29 euros.*
false [fɔːls]	falsch	*Is the answer true or false?*
south [saʊθ]	Süden	*Hastings is in the south of England.*

Focus 2

hometown ['həʊm,taʊn]	Heimatort	*Bonn is my home town. I was born there.*
east [iːst]	Ost/en	*Dresden is in east Germany.*
exactly [ɪg'zæktli]	genau	*Where is that exactly? – Near Bonn.*
cathedral [kə'θiːdrəl]	Dom, Kathedrale	*St. Paul's Cathedral is beautiful.*
bridge [brɪdʒ]	Brücke	*I would love to see the Golden Gate bridge.*
(to) **sound** [saʊnd]	klingen	*That sounds good.*
any ['eni]	*wird oft nicht übersetzt,* irgendwelche; etwas	*Are there any mountains in Germany?*
nearby [,nɪə'baɪ]	in der Nähe	*Is there an airport nearby?*
not any [nɒt 'eni]	kein/e	*There aren't any flowers in our classroom.*
except [ɪk'sept]	außer	*I'm free every day except Wednesday.*
museum [mju'ziːəm]	Museum	*Would you like to go to museum at the weekend?*
historic building [hɪ,stɒrɪk 'bɪldɪŋ]	historisches Gebäude	*Are there any historic buildings in your town?*
river ['rɪvə]	Fluss	*Many cities are built along rivers.*
university [,juːnɪ'vɜːsəti]	Universität	*Dublin has a wonderful university.*
club [klʌb]	Klub, Verein	*My sister is in a football club.*
well-known [,wel'nəʊn]	sehr bekannt	*Siemens is a well-known company.*

poster ['pəʊstə]	Plakat	*That's my face on the poster.*
slogan ['sləʊgən]	Slogan, Werbespruch	*Does your company have a slogan?*
(to) **divide** [dɪ'vaɪd]	teilen	*Divide the cake into four pieces.*
whole [hɜul]	ganze/r/s	*Isn't it wonderful? Two whole weeks away!*
(to) **collect** [kə'lekt]	sammeln	*He collects coins.*
should [ʃʊd]	sollte/n, solltest, solltet	*You should stop smoking.*

Planning

What shall we do?	Was sollen wir tun?
Will you ..., please?	Würden Sie / Würdest du bitte ...
How about ... ?	Wie wäre es mit ... ?
That's a good idea!	Das ist eine gute Idee!
No, I think ... is better.	Nein, ich glaube, ... ist besser.

nowadays ['naʊədeɪz]	heutzutage	*Everything is so different nowadays.*
mobile ['məʊbaɪl]	mobil, beweglich	*Nowadays it's very important to be mobile.*
(to) **get married** [get 'mærɪd]	heiraten	*I don't want to get married in church.*
(to) **grow up, grew up** [ˌgrəʊ 'ʌp], [gru: 'ʌp]	aufwachsen	*Where did you grow up? – In Poland.*
(to) **die** [daɪ]	sterben	*My grandfather died last year. He was 88.*
(to) **get retrained** [get rɪ'treɪnd]	eine Umschulung machen	*When I lost my job I got retrained.*
(to) **leave school** [li:v 'sku:l]	von der Schule abgehen	*She left school when she was sixteen.*
(to) **get divorced** [get dɪ'vɔ:st]	sich scheiden lassen	*My brother got divorced two years ago.*
(to) **retire** [rɪ'taɪə]	in den Ruhestand gehen	*When I retire I want to go to Alabama.*
(to) **go abroad** [gəʊ ə'brɔ:d]	ins Ausland gehen/fahren	
(to) **have children** [həv 'tʃɪldrən]	Kinder kriegen	! have children ~~get children~~
life history [laɪf 'hɪstri]	Lebensgeschichte	
(to) **lead, led** [li:d, led]	führen	*You lead such an interesting life.*

(to) **add** [æd]	hinzufügen	*Would you like to add any ideas?*

Magazine

handball ['hændbɔːl]	Handball	*Handball is not as popular as football.*
first class ticket [ˌfɜːst 'klɑːs ˌtɪkɪt]	Fahrkarte für die erste Klasse	*Do you sometimes buy a first class ticket?*
second class ticket [ˌsekənd 'klɑːs ˌtɪkɪt]	Fahrkarte für die zweite Klasse	*I normally buy a second class ticket.*
noisy ['nɔɪzi]	laut, lärmend	*Our neighbours are very noisy.*
main road [meɪn 'rəʊd]	Hauptstraße	*My house is on the main road, so it's really noisy.*
playground ['pleɪgraʊnd]	Spielplatz	
twentysomething [ˌtwenti'sʌmθɪŋ]	jemand in den Zwanzigern	*Berlin is a city for twentysomethings.*
rich [rɪtʃ]	reich, wohlhabend	*I don't know many rich people.*
anything ['eniθɪŋ]	irgendetwas	*Is there anything I can do for you?*
anything like that	etwas dergleichen	
tired ['taɪəd]	müde	*I'm tired and I want to go home.*
next door [nekst 'dɔː]	nebenan	*My girlfriend lives next door.*
Worse was to come.	Schlimmeres stand noch bevor.	*... and that wasn't the end. Worse was to come.*
key [kiː]	Schlüssel	*I couldn't find my keys.*
suitcase, case ['suːtkeɪs, keɪs]	Koffer	*What's in the suitcase?*
could [kʊd]	*Vergangenheitsform von* can	*I could swim very well I was a child.*
couldn't [kʊdnt]	*verneinte Form von* could	*The teacher couldn't come to class yesterday.*
(to) **open** ['əʊpən]	öffnen	*Open the window, please.*
carefully ['keəflɪ]	sorgfältig	*I opened the bag carefully.*
(to) **believe** [bɪ'liːv]	glauben	*Can you believe it?*
anyone ['enɪwʌn]	irgendjemand	*Can anyone hear me?*
anywhere ['enɪweə]	irgendwo	*I couldn't see anyone anywhere.*
present [preznt]	Geschenk	*I got lots of birthday presents this year.*

gallon ['gælən]	Gallone	*My car needs gallons of petrol every day.*
pint [paɪnt]	Pint	*Two pints of beer, please!*

Story

seminar ['semɪnɑː]	Seminar, Fachtagung	*Did you enjoy the seminar?*
a number of [ə 'nʌmbər əf]	eine Reihe von	*They asked me a number of questions.*
organization [ˌɔːgənaɪ'zeɪʃn]	Organisation	*The UN is an international organization.*
heard [hɜːd]	*Vergangenheitsform von* hear	*I heard about your new job.*
(to) **hear a rumour** [ˌhɪər ə 'ruːmə]	ein Gerücht hören	*Never listen to rumours.*
takeover ['teɪkəʊvə]	Übernahme, Fusion	*Tara heard a rumour of a takeover.*
(to) **be worried** [bi 'wʌrid]	besorgt/beunruhigt sein	*She was worried because her daughter was on a party.*
note [nəʊt]	Notiz	*Write a short note, not a long letter.*
(I) might be late home.	Könnte sein, dass ich spät nach Hause komme.	*I might be late home this evening.*
(to) **wait** [weɪt]	warten	*Wait for me!*
Don't wait up for me.	Du brauchst nicht aufzubleiben.	*Go to bed. Don't wait up for me.*

Lucky you! — Sie/Du Glückliche/r!

UNIT 10

Focus 1

(to) **describe** [dɪ'skraɪb]	beschreiben	*Can you describe your teacher?*
What sort of ...? [wɒt 'sɔːt əv]	was für (ein/e) ...?	*What sort of books do you like?*
character ['kærəktə]	Person	*She's such a funny character.*
situation [ˌsɪtʃu'eɪʃn]	Situation, Lage	*What would you do in my situation?*

easy-going [ˌiːzi ˈgəʊɪŋ]	unkompliziert	*She's an easy-going person.*
serious [ˈsɪəriəs]	ernst(haft)	*Clowns are usually very serious people.*
(to) **be lucky** [bɪ ˈlʌki]	Glück haben	*I'm so lucky I found a job.*
musical [ˈmjuːzɪkl]	musikalisch	*He's very musical: He sings in the shower!*
lively [ˈlaɪvli]	lebendig, lebhaft	*She's a very lively child.*
untidy [ʌnˈtaɪdi]	unordentlich, unaufgeräumt	*She's not untidy, just creative.*
organized [ˈɔːgənaɪzd]	gut organisiert	*Is Ben an organized person?*
funny [ˈfʌni]	komisch, lustig	*Do you like Mr Bean? – Yes, he's very funny.*
quiet [ˈkwaɪət]	still, ruhig	*My brother is a very quiet person.*
(to) **be unlucky** [bɪ ʌnˈlʌki]	Pech haben	*Ben is an unlucky person. He often misses the bus.*
a morning person [ə ˈmɔːnɪŋ ˌpɜːsn]	kein Morgenmuffel	*She's definitely not a morning person.*
sad [sæd]	traurig	*What a sad song.*
calm [kɑːm]	ruhig, gelassen	*She is a very relaxed and calm person.*
talkative [ˈtɔːkətɪv]	redselig, gesprächig	*My aunt is a very talkative person.*

Discussing and conversation

I don't think …	Ich glaube nicht, dass …
For me …	Für mich …
Do you think so?	Meinen/Glauben Sie?
She's/He's more interesting than …	Sie/Er ist interessanter als …

stress [stres]	Betonung	*Listen for the main stress.*
island [ˈaɪlənd]	Insel	*Would you like to live on an island?*
hat [hæt]	Hut	*She wears wonderful hats.*
Lord of the Rings [ˌlɔːd əv ðə ˈrɪŋz]	Herr der Ringe *(Buchtitel)*	*You must be a "Lord of the Rings" fan.*
long-distance walking [lɒŋˈdɪstəns ˌwɔːkɪŋ]	Wandern	*We often go long-distance walking in summer.*
mug [mʌg]	Becher, große Tasse	*I like to drink a big mug of hot chocolate.*

autumn ['ɔ:təm]	Herbst	*I love autumn.*
peanut butter ['pi:nʌt ˌbʌtə]	Erdnussbutter	*Toasts with peanut butter are wonderful.*
clothes [kləʊðz]	Kleider, Kleidung	*The children have nice clothes.*
season [si:zn]	Jahreszeit	*Summer is the most beautiful season of the year.*
soap opera ['səʊp ɒprə]	Seifenoper	*My favourite soap opera is Lindenstraße.*
(to) **spend free time** [spend ˌfri: 'taɪm]	Freizeit verbringen	*How do you spend your free time?*
classical music [ˌklæsɪkl 'mju:zɪk]	klassische Musik	*They enjoy listening to classical music.*
above [ə'bʌv]	oben	*Look above your head.*
(to) **have** (**sth**) **in common** [ɪn 'kɒmən]	etwas gemeinsam haben	*We have a lot of things in common.*
both [bəʊθ]	beide	*They are both very athletic.*
neither … nor … ['naɪðər nɔ:]	weder … noch …	*Neither Sue nor Jo like sport.*

Focus 2

(to) **use** [ju:z]	gebrauchen, benutzen	*Could I use your telephone, please?*
per day/hour/week [pə 'deɪ, 'aʊə, 'wi:k]	pro Tag/Stunde/Woche	*How many texts do you send per day?*
business partner ['bɪznəs ˌpɑ:tnə]	Geschäftspartner/in	*Our business partners come from Toronto.*
(to) **arrange** [ə'reɪndʒ]	abmachen, vereinbaren	*My mother likes to arrange things for me.*
I see. [aɪ 'si:]	Ich verstehe./Ach so.	*Paco is in a meeting. – I see.*
line [laɪn]	(Telefon-)Leitung	*Hello? – I'm sorry, there was a problem with the line.*
It's all right. [ɪts ɔ:l 'raɪt]	Ist schon in Ordnung/gut.	*It's all right. = It's OK.*
(to) **call** [kɔ:l]	anrufen	*I'll call back later.*
(to) **dial** ['daɪəl]	wählen	*He dialled the wrong number.*
(to) **act out sth** [ˌækt 'aʊt]	etwas vorspielen	*Can you act out the dialogue?*

Telephoning

Beginn eines Telefongesprächs/Sie möchten mit jemandem sprechen:

This is (Ben Murphy) in (London).	Hier ist (Ben Murphy) in (London).
Hello, is that (Paco)?	Hallo, ist dort (Paco)?
Can I speak to (Paco), please?	Kann ich bitte (mit) (Paco) sprechen?
I'd like to speak to (Paco), please.	Ich möchte bitte (mit) (Paco) sprechen.
Certainly.	Selbstverständlich.

Sie reagieren auf einen Anruf:

This is ... speaking.	Hier ist ...
How can I help you?	Wie kann ich Ihnen helfen?
Just a moment, please.	Einen Augenblick, bitte.
I'm afraid (Paco) is not here.	(Paco) ist leider nicht da.

Bei Funkproblemen und gestörten Leitungen:

Hello? Can you hear me?	Hallo? Können Sie mich hören?
Hello? Are you still there?	Hallo? Sind Sie noch dran?
I'm sorry, there was a problem with the line.	Es tut mir Leid, die Leitung war gestört.

Der gewünschte Gesprächspartner ist nicht erreichbar:

Hold on.	Bleiben Sie / Bleib dran.
I'll connect you.	Ich verbinde (Sie).
I'm afraid there's no answer.	Es geht leider niemand ans Telefon.
That's a pity!	Das ist schade!
Can I take a message?	Kann ich etwas ausrichten?
Do you want to leave a message?	Möchten Sie eine Nachricht hinterlassen?
I'll call back later.	Ich rufe später zurück.
What shall I tell her/him?	Was soll ich ihr/ihm sagen?
I'll tell her/him you called.	Ich sage ihr/ihm, dass Sie angerufen haben.
I'll give her/him your message.	Ich leite Ihre Nachricht an sie/ihn weiter.
I'll see that she/he gets the message.	Ich sorge dafür, dass sie/er die Nachricht bekommt.

Focus 3

(to) **let** [let]	lassen	*Let me help you.*
bubble ['bʌbl]	(Sprech-)Blase	
(to) **declare** [dɪ'kleə]	verzollen	*Go straight through if you have nothing to declare.*
immediately [ɪ'mi:diətli]	unverzüglich	*Please phone him immediately.*
baggage reclaim [ˌbægɪdʒ 'ri:kleɪm]	Gepäckausgabe	*Where's the baggage reclaim?*
pocket ['pɒkɪt]	Tasche	*What's in your pocket?*
customs ['kʌstəmz]	Zoll	*They stopped us at customs last year.*

At the airport

Meeting someone

How are you?	Wie geht es Ihnen/dir?
Fine, thanks.	Danke, gut.
Nice to meet you (too).	Schön, Sie/dich zu treffen.
How was your flight?	Wie war Ihr/dein Flug?
Great, thanks.	Hervorragend.
The plane was only half full.	Das Flugzeug war nur halb voll.
Let me take your bag.	Lassen Sie mich Ihre / Lass mich deine Tasche nehmen.
Welcome to …	Willkommen in …

Saying goodbye

It was nice meeting you.	Es war schön, Sie/dich zu treffen.
It was nice to see you again.	Es war schön, Sie/dich mal wieder zu sehen.
Enjoy your trip.	Gute Reise.
Have a good flight.	Guten Flug.
I hope to see you again soon.	Hoffentlich sehe ich Sie/dich bald wieder.

Magazine

TRANSCRIPT

That's a pity. [ðæts ə 'pɪti]	Das ist schade.	*No more tickets? That's a pity.*
foot, feet [fʊt], [fi:t]	Fuß, Füße	*I bath my feet after a long day at work.*
as soon as [əz 'su:n əz]	sobald	*I'll speak to him as soon as soon as he comes in.*

art [ɑːt]	Kunst	*Are you interested in art?*
art gallery ['ɑːt ˌɡæləri]	Kunstgalerie	*I love visiting art galleries at the weekend.*
a few [ə 'fjuː]	einige, ein paar	*Would you like to see a few of my paintings?*
personality [ˌpɜːsə'næləti]	Persönlichkeit	*Can you describe your personality?*

colour *(BE)*, **color** *(AE)* ['kʌlə]	Farbe	**purple** ['pɜːpl]	lila
black [blæk]	schwarz	**blue** [bluː]	blau
brown [braʊn]	braun	**green** [ɡriːn]	grün
orange ['ɒrɪndʒ]	orange	**grey** [ɡreɪ]	grau
yellow ['jeləʊ]	gelb	**white** [waɪt]	weiß
red [red]	rot	**turquoise** ['tɜːkwɔɪz]	türkis
pink [pɪŋk]	pink, rosa		

(to) **feel, felt** [fiːl], [felt]	(sich) fühlen	*How do you feel? – Great!*
(to) **feel your best** [fiːl jə best]	sich am besten fühlen	*When do you feel your best?*
during ['djʊərɪŋ]	während	*She meets him during the afternoon.*
head up [hed 'ʌp]	mit erhobenem Kopf; Kopf hoch	*Head up! It's not so bad.*
spring [sprɪŋ]	Frühling	*What do you do in spring?*
loud [laʊd]	laut	*You're too loud. Be quiet.*
loud entrance [laʊd 'entrəns]	lauter Auftritt	*She makes a loud entrance at parties.*
(to) **hope** [həʊp]	hoffen	*I hope you're well.*
dark [dɑːk]	dunkel	*This room is very dark.*
light [laɪt]	hell	*Her new suit is a light blue.*
(to) **add up** [ˌæd 'ʌp]	zusammenzählen	*Add up your points, please.*

point [pɔɪnt]	Punkt	*You get one point for every correct answer.*
shy [ʃaɪ]	schüchtern	*I was always very shy.*
nervous ['nɜːvəs]	nervös	*Don't be so nervous. Everything will be OK.*
(to) **make a decision** [ˌmeɪk ə dɪ'sɪʒn]	eine Entscheidung treffen	*It's not easy to make big decisions.*
careful ['keəfl]	vorsichtig	*Be careful, there's a car coming.*
(to) **react** [ri'ækt]	reagieren	*I sometimes react too quickly.*
attention [ə'tenʃn]	Aufmerksamkeit	*She's the centre of my attention.*
charming ['tʃɑːmɪŋ]	charmant, reizend	*He's such a charming man.*
impulsive [ɪm'pʌlsɪv]	impulsiv	*Darling, don't be so impulsive.*

Story

cooperation [kəʊˌɒpə'reɪʃn]	Zusammenarbeit	*We need a cooperation partner for our business.*
project ['prɒdʒekt]	Projekt	*We worked together on a big project.*
agent ['eɪdʒənt]	Vertreter/in	*I bought the tickets from my local travel agent.*
might [maɪt]	könnte/n; könntest, könntet	*I might go to England this year. I'm not sure.*
soon [suːn]	bald	*See you soon!*
local ['ləʊkl]	lokal, einheimisch	*She's the manager of a local art gallery.*
paper ['peɪpə]	Zeitung	*He writes for a local paper.*
teammate ['tiːmmeɪt]	Teammitglied	*She's my teammate.*
unusually [ʌn'juːʒuəli]	ungewöhnlich(erweise)	*He has unusually big ears.*
(to) **confront** [kən'frʌnt]	konfrontieren	*She confronted Steve with the news.*
(to) **admit** [əd'mɪt]	zugeben, (ein)gestehen	*Admit it. You have a problem.*
(to) **have an affair** [həv ən ə'feə]	ein Verhältnis haben	*Steve admitted having an affair.*
(to) **move out** [ˌmuːv 'aʊt]	ausziehen	*He moved out of their old flat.*
bad news [bæd 'njuːz]	schlechte Nachrichten	*You're ill? That's bad news.*

I'm really sorry.
– Oh, don't worry.

Es tut mir wirklich Leid.
– Oh, machen Sie sich / mach dir keine Sorgen.

UNIT 11

Focus 1

(to) **be out and about** [bi ˌaʊt ənd əˈbaʊt]	unterwegs sein	*She's often out and about.*
(to) **prepare** [prɪˈpeə]	(sich) vorbereiten	*I have to prepare a meeting for tomorrow.*

adapter [əˈdæptə]	Adapter	**paper** [ˈpeɪpə]	Papier
battery [ˈbætəri]	Batterie	**pen** [pen]	Füller, Kugelschreiber
brush [brʌʃ]	Bürste	**phrasebook** [ˈfreɪzbʊk]	*Buch mit Redewendungen*
camera [ˈkæmərə]	Fotoapparat, Kamera	**pullover** [ˈpʊləʊvə]	Pullover
comb [kəʊm]	Kamm	**sandals** [ˈsændlz]	Sandalen
evening dress [ˈiːvnɪŋ dres]	Abendkleid	**scarf** [skɑːf]	Schal
glove [glʌv]	Handschuh	(a pair of) **scissors** [ˈsɪzəz]	Schere
guidebook [ˈgaɪdbʊk]	Reiseführer	**shampoo** [ʃæmˈpuː]	Shampoo
hairdryer [ˈheədraɪə]	Fön	(a pair of) **sunglasses** [ˈsʌnglɑːsɪz]	Sonnenbrille
map [mæp]	Stadtplan	**sunscreen** [ˈsʌnskriːn]	Sonnenschutzmittel
medicine [ˈmedsn]	Medizin, Medikament(e)	**umbrella** [ʌmˈbrelə]	(Regen-)Schirm
MP3-player [ˌem piː ˈθriː ˌpleɪə]	MP3-Player	**walking shoes** [ˈwɔːkɪŋ ʃuːz]	Wanderschuhe
novel [ˈnɒvl]	Roman		

(to) **explain** [ɪkˈspleɪn]	erklären	*Could you explain that again?*
wouldn't [ˈwʊdnt]	*verneinte Form von* would	*I wouldn't take my evening dress on holiday.*

luggage ['lʌgɪdʒ]	Gepäck	*He has a lot of luggage.*
hand luggage ['hænd lʌgɪdʒ]	Handgepäck	*I always have something to read in my hand luggage.*

Focus 2

(to) **cost** [kɒst]	kosten	*How much did the hotel cost?*
(to) **look for sth** ['lʊk fə]	(nach) etwas suchen	*I'm looking for a map of Barcelona.*
compact ['kɒmpækt]	kompakt	*I bought a compact dictionary for my holiday.*
(to) **have a look at sth** [ˌhəv ə 'lʊk ət]	sich etwas anschauen	*Can I have a look at this?*
schoolbook ['sku:lbʊk]	Schulbuch	*Do you still have your old schoolbooks?*
price [praɪs]	(Kauf-)Preis	*It was a special price, only for friends.*
(to) **try sth on** [ˌtraɪ ˌsʌmθɪŋ 'ɒn]	etwas anprobieren	*Can I try it on?*

TRANSCRIPT

Shopping phrases

Can I have a look, please?	Darf ich mich bitte mal umsehen?
How can I help you?	Wie kann ich Ihnen helfen?
I'd like …	Ich hätte/möchte gern …
Do you have … ?	Haben Sie … ?
I'm looking for …	Ich suche …
I'm just looking.	Ich sehe mich nur mal um.
How much is it?	Was kostet es?
How much are they?	Was kosten sie?
How much does it cost?	Was kostet es?
How much do they cost?	Was kosten sie?
I'll take it/them.	Ich nehme es/sie.

can [kæn]	Dose	*Can I have a can of beer, please?*
survey ['sɜ:veɪ]	Umfrage, Übersicht	*Some companies do surveys on the phone.*
(to) **keep, kept** [ki:p], [kept]	behalten	*Keep your lists.*
lesson ['lesn]	Unterrichtsstunde	*We have two English lessons per week.*
petrol ['petrəl]	Benzin	*My car needs a lot of petrol.*
health-food shop ['helθ fu:d ˌʃɒp]	Naturkostladen	*Is there a health food shop near your house?*

petrol station ['petrəl ˌsteɪʃn]	Tankstelle	*Petrol stations are good for late night shopping.*
special offer [ˌspeʃl 'ɒfə]	Sonderangebot	*They had a special offer at Harrods.*

Focus 3

T

kind [kaɪnd]	freundlich, nett	*My neighbours are kind people.*
(to) **ask the way** [ˌɑːsk ðə 'weɪ]	nach dem Weg fragen	*The man asked for the way to the city centre.*
spontaneous [spɒn'teɪniəs]	spontan	*Can you give a spontaneous answer?*
decision [dɪ'sɪʒn]	Entscheidung	*It was a spontaneous decision to meet you.*
polite [pə'laɪt]	höflich	*Always be polite in England.*
intonation [ˌɪntə'neɪʃn]	Tonfall	
palace ['pæləs]	Palast	
road [rəʊd]	(Land-)Straße	
square ['skweə]	Platz	

(!) Im Englischen sind Plätze meistens squares:
Palace square
~~Palace place~~

Asking the way

Can you tell me the way to … ?	Können Sie mir sagen, wie ich zum/nach … komme?
How do I get there?	Wie komme ich dorthin?
Go along here.	Gehen Sie hier entlang.
Turn left/right.	Biegen Sie nach links/rechts ab.
Go past (the bank).	Gehen Sie/Geh an (der Bank) vorbei.
Turn right …	Biegen Sie nach rechts ab …
… into Crendon Road.	… in die Crendon Road.
It's the second street on the left/right.	Es ist die zweite Straße links/rechts.
Turn left/right at the corner.	Biegen Sie an der Ecke links/rechts ab.
Go straight on at the traffic lights.	Gehen Sie/Geh an der Ampel geradeaus.
It's along there …	Es ist dort entlang …
… on the left/right.	… auf der linken/rechten Seite.
Take the …	Nehmen Sie die …
street on the left/right.	Straße links/rechts.
It's this way, not that way.	Es ist in dieser Richtung, nicht in der.
It's near …	Es ist in der Nähe von …

theatre ['θɪətə]	Theater	*My uncle worked in the theatre. He was an actor.*
fine arts [faɪn 'ɑːts]	schöne Künste	*I studied fine arts at university.*
post office ['pəʊst ˌɒfɪs]	Postamt	*I always have to wait long in the post office.*
central ['sentrəl]	zentral, Zentral-	*My flat is very central – there are many shops nearby.*
direction [də'rekʃn]	Richtung, Weg	*This is the wrong direction. We must go back.*
(to) **give sb directions**	jdm den Weg beschreiben	*Can you give me directions for the airport, please?*

Magazine

TRANSCRIPT

stamp [stæmp]	Briefmarke	*How much is a stamp to Canada?*
himself [hɪm'self]	sich (selbst), er selbst	*Jack wants to buy a T-shirt for himself.*
in the end [ˌɪn ði 'end]	zum Schluss, schließlich	*Did you buy the jacket in the end?*
shop assistant ['ʃɒp əˌsɪstənt]	Verkäufer/in	*The shop assistant was friendly.*
at the moment ['məʊmənt]	im Moment	*We're just looking at the moment.*
mine [maɪn]	meine/r/s	*These books are mine.*
two of those [ˌtuː əf 'ðəʊz]	zwei davon	*Can I have two of those, please?*
That's not bad.	Das ist nicht schlecht.	
Don't be silly.	Red keinen Unsinn.	
(to) **wear, wore** [weə], [wɔː]	*(Kleidung)* tragen	! She wears a red dress and carries a black handbag.
(to) **carry** ['kæri]	in der Hand tragen	
toy [tɔɪ]	Spielzeug	*My boyfriend still plays with toys.*
mouse, mice [maʊs], [maɪs]	Maus, Mäuse	
arm [ɑːm]	Arm	*Wow, you have long arms!*
a bit [ə 'bɪt]	ein bisschen	*He's a bit too young to watch horror films.*
mouse mat ['maʊsmæt]	Mauspad	
in cash [ɪn 'kæʃ]	in bar	*I'd like to pay in cash.*
medium ['miːdɪəm]	mittel(groß)	*What size are you? – Medium.*

changing room ['tʃeɪndʒɪŋ ruːm]	Umkleideraum, -kabine	*Excuse me. Where is the changing room?*
(to) **take** [teɪk]	akzeptieren	*Do you take credit cards?*
size [saɪz]	Größe	
comfortable ['kʌmftəbl]	bequem	! Achtung, falscher Freund: Englisch comfortable ist nicht gleich deutsch „komfortabel".
quality ['kwɒləti]	Qualität	
value ['væljuː]	Wert	
good value [gʊd 'væljuː]	preisgünstig	*It's good value.*
(to) **go past sth** [gəʊ 'pɑːst]	an etwas vorbeigehen	*Go past the restaurant and you'll see the pub.*
stressful ['stresfl]	anstrengend, stressig	*Travelling can be stressful.*
trouble ['trʌbl]	Ärger	*My parents had a lot of trouble with me.*
simple ['sɪmpl]	einfach	*This game is very simple.*
rule [ruːl]	Regel	*There are not many rules in English grammar.*
vacation *(AE)* [və'keɪʃnv]	Urlaub, Ferien	*Let's go on vacation.*
important [ɪm'pɔːtnt]	wichtig	*Do you have all the important things you need?*
side pocket ['saɪd ˌpɒkɪt]	Seitentasche	*Put the bottle in the side pocket.*
backpack ['bækpæk]	Rucksack	*Don't leave your backpack alone!*
bottom ['bɒtəm]	Boden	*My keys are always at the bottom of my bag.*
easy ['iːzi]	leicht	*It's so easy to forget things.*
(to) **tie** [taɪ]	(an)binden	*Tie a cloth to your luggage.*
bright [braɪt]	hell, kräftig *(Farbe)*	*The sun is very bright today.*
coloured *(BE)* ['kʌləd]	farbig	! coloured (BE) colored (AE)
cloth [klɒθ]	Tuch, Stoff	
mosquito bite [məs'kiːtəʊ baɪt]	Mückenstich	
lemon juice ['lemən dʒuːs]	Zitronensaft	*Fresh lemon juice is perfect on a hot summer's day.*

TRANSCRIPT

chain store ['tʃeɪn stɔː]	Filiale (einer Kette)	Achtung, falscher Freund: warehouse = Lager; department store = Warenhaus
department store [dɪ'pɑːtmənt stɔː]	Kauf-, Warenhaus	
shopping mall ['ʃɒpɪŋ mɔːl]	Einkaufszentrum	
deli ['deli]	Delikatessengeschäft	*There's a great deli on the corner.*

I think we're lost. Let's ask someone the way.

Ich glaube, wir haben uns verirrt. Fragen wir jemanden nach dem Weg.

UNIT 12

Focus 1

(to) **look back** [ˌlʊk 'bæk]	zurückblicken	*Looking back, I think this was good.*
(to) **look ahead** [ˌlʊk ə'hed]	vorausschauen	*I'm looking ahead to the project.*
beginning [bɪ'gɪnɪŋ]	Anfang	*He felt very romantic at the beginning.*
at the beginning [ˌət ðə bɪ'gɪnɪŋ]	am Anfang	*We met Tara and Ben at the beginning.*
met [met]	*Vergangenheitsform von* meet	*I met my wife six years ago.*
type of ['taɪp əv]	Art von	*What type of holiday do you like?*

Focus 2

adventure [əd'ventʃə]	Abenteuer	*Our last holiday was an adventure.*
tax advisor ['tæks ədvaɪzə]	Steuerberater/in	*I need a tax advisor.*
dentist ['dentɪst]	Zahnarzt, Zahnärztin	*I don't like going to the dentist.*
(to) **be free** [bi 'friː]	Zeit haben	*When are you free?*
arrangement [ə'reɪndʒmənt]	Vereinbarung	*We made an arrangement to meet in Paris.*
(to) **make an arrangement**	eine Vereinbarung treffen	*Shall we make an arrange-ment to meet at 10 a.m.?*

over the weekend [ˌəʊvə ðə ˌwiːk'end]	übers Wochenende	*I was in London over the weekend.*
help [help]	Hilfe	*Tell me if you need help.*
computer system [kəm'pjuːtə sɪstəm]	Computersystem	*Not again! Another problem with the computer system.*
IT [aɪ 'tiː]	*Abk. von* information technology, IT	*She works in IT.*
far [fɑː]	weit (entfernt)	*How far is it? – 20 kilometres.*
(to) **underline** [ˌʌndə'laɪn]	unterstreichen	*I underlined the most important information.*
future ['fjuːtʃə]	Zukunft	*Do you have plans for the future?*
schedule ['ʃedjuːl]	Zeitplan	*I have a busy schedule next week.*
opera ['ɒprə]	Oper	*I love going to the opera.*
(to) **go to the opera** [ˌgəʊ tə ði 'ɒprə]	in die Oper gehen	*Are you going to the opera with me?*
(to) **work late** [wɜːk 'leɪt]	lange arbeiten	*Working late is not good for your health.*
(to) **babysit** ['beɪbisɪt]	babysitten	*Can you babysit my daughter at the weekend?*

Making arrangements

When are you free?	Wann haben Sie / hast du Zeit?
Let's say (Wednesday).	Lassen Sie uns / Lass uns (Mittwoch) sagen.
Is (Wednesday) possible?	Wäre (Mittwoch) möglich?
Are you free on (Wednesday)?	Haben Sie / Hast du Zeit am (Mittwoch)?
I'm sorry I can't make it on (Wednesday).	Es tut mir Leid, aber am (Mittwoch) schaffe ich es nicht.
OK then, let's say (Thursday).	In Ordnung. Dann lassen Sie uns / lass uns (Donnerstag) sagen.
Yes, that's fine.	Ja, das klappt gut.

Focus 3

(to) **sum up** [ˌsʌm 'ʌp]	zusammenfassen	*To sum up, I really enjoyed the time with you.*
(to) **think of sth/sb** ['θɪŋk əf]	sich etw ausdenken, an etwas/jdn denken	*I often think of her.*
client ['klaɪənt]	Kunde/Kundin	*I'm meeting a client from Brazil tomorrow.*
word order ['wɜːd ɔːdə]	Wortstellung	*Is this the right word order?*

basic ['beɪsɪk]	wesentlich	*What are the basic facts in that story?*
(to) **understand, understood** [ʌndə'stænd, ʌndə'stʊd]	verstehen	*Do you understand French?*
(to) **ask for help** [ˌɑːsk fə 'help]	um Hilfe bitten	*Can I ask you for help?*
What else? [wɒt 'els]	Was noch?	*What else can you tell me about that day?*

Working on a project

Let's …	Lassen Sie / Lasst uns …
Let's write a sentence about …	Schreiben wir einen Satz über …
I have an idea.	Ich habe eine Idee.
I think you're right.	Ich glaube, Sie haben / du hast Recht.
No, I don't think so.	Nein, ich bin anderer Meinung.
Shall we … ?	Sollen wir … ?
That's a great question.	Das ist eine gute Frage.
Are you sure … is correct?	Sind Sie sich / Bist du dir sicher, dass … stimmt?
I'll write that one down.	Das schreibe ich auf.

Story

I think so. [ˌaɪ 'θɪŋk səʊ]	Ich glaube schon.	*Does Ben like Tara? – I think so.*
sang [sæŋ]	*Vergangenheitsform von* sing	*She sang a song about love.*
That was me.	Das war ich.	
stuff [stʌf]	*umgangssprachlich:* Zeugs	*I don't know how you can eat that stuff.*
What sort of stuff do you play?	Was spielen Sie / spielst du denn?	
cover band ['kʌvə bænd]	Coverband	
…, you know. [ju 'nəʊ]	…, wissen Sie / weißt du?	
Just for fun.	Nur zum Spaß.	
dramatic [drə'mætɪk]	dramatisch	
by mistake [baɪ mɪ'steɪk]	aus Versehen	*I ate your chocolate by mistake.*
(to) **breathe down the phone**	ins Telefon hauchen	

! *you know* wird aus kommunikativen Gründen angehängt. Es ist keine Frage, und Sie müssen darauf auch nicht antworten.

Magazine

treasure ['treʒə]	Schatz	*Can you find the treasure?*
treasure hunt ['treʒə hʌnt]	Schatzsuche	*Children love treasure hunts.*
chain [tʃeɪn]	Kette	

Quick Check 3

TRANSCRIPT

brackets ['brækɪts]	Klammern	*Always read what's in the brackets.*
armchair ['ɑ:mtʃeə]	Sessel	*I'd like to sit in my arm-chair and watch TV!*
ears ['ɪəz]	Ohren	*... and the monster had really big, green ears.*
(to) **get in** [get 'ɪn]	ankommen, landen	*When does your train get into Berlin?*
(to) **be available** [bi ə'veɪləbl]	(am Telefon) zu sprechen sein	*I'm not available for anybody this morning.*
heavy ['hevi]	schwer *(Gewicht)*	*My head feels so heavy I'm really tired.*
(to) **book** [bʊk]	buchen, vorbestellen, reservieren	*I've booked a table at the restaurant.*
(to) **be allergic to sth** [bi ə'lɜ:dʒɪk tə]	gegen etwas allergisch sein	*My brother is allergic to strawberries.*
diet [ˌdaɪət]	Diät	*She's always on a diet.*
soup [su:p]	Suppe	*I'd like a vegetable soup, please.*
paté ['pæteɪ]	Pastete	*This paté is wonderful.*
olive ['ɒlɪv]	Olive	*Do you prefer black or green olives?*
still [stɪl]	still *(Wasser)*	*Would you like still or sparkling mineral water?*
sparkling ['spɑ:klɪŋ]	sprudelnd *(Wasser)*	*I'd like a glass of sparkling wine, please.*
gossip ['gɒsɪp]	Klatsch, Tratsch	*Did you hear any inter-esting gossip?*

Take care of yourself!
See you next term.

Passen Sie gut auf sich /
Pass gut auf dich auf!
Bis zum nächsten Semester.

Place Names and Nationalities

America	[ə'merɪkə]	Amerika
American	[ə'merɪkən]	amerikanisch
Amsterdam	[ˌæmstə'dæm]	Amsterdam
Australia	[ɒ'streɪliə]	Australien
Austria	['ɒstriə]	Österreich
Austrian	['ɒstriən]	österreichisch
Bangkok	[bæŋ'kɒk]	*Hauptstadt Thailands*
Barcelona	[ˌbɑːsɪ'ləʊnə]	Barcelona
Bavaria	[bə'veəriə]	Bayern
Berlin	[bɜː'lɪn]	Berlin
Berne	[bɜːn]	Bern
Bolivia	[bə'lɪvɪə]	Bolivien
Bondi Beach	['bɒndaɪ biːtʃ]	*Strand nahe Sydney*
Brazil	[brə'zɪl]	Brasilien
Britain	['brɪtən]	Großbritannien
British	['brɪtɪʃ]	britisch
Calcutta	[kæl'kʌtə]	*drittgrößte Stadt Indiens*
Canada	['kænədə]	Kanada
Canadian	[kə'neɪdiən]	kanadisch
Canberra	['kænbərə]	*Hauptstadt Australiens*
China	['tʃaɪnə]	China
Chinese	[tʃaɪ'niːz]	chinesisch
Cologne	[kə'ləʊn]	Köln
(the river) Danube	['dænjuːb]	Donau
Dresden	['drezdən]	Dresden
Dublin	['dʌblɪn]	*Hauptstadt der Republik Irland*
Edinburgh	['edɪnbərə]	*Hauptstadt Schottlands*
Eiffel Tower	[ˌaɪfl'taʊə]	Eiffelturm
England	['ɪŋglənd]	England
English	['ɪŋglɪʃ]	englisch
European	[ˌjʊərə'piːən]	europäisch
Finland	['fɪnlənd]	Finnland
Florence	['flɒrəns]	Florenz
France	[frɑːns]	Frankreich
French	[frentʃ]	französisch
Galapagos Islands	[gə'læpəgəs ˌaɪləndz]	*Inselgruppe im Pazifischen Ozean (Ecuador)*
Galicia	[gə'lɪsiə]	Galizien
Geneva	[dʒə'niːvə]	Genf
German	['dʒɜːmən]	deutsch
Germany	['dʒɜːməni]	Deutschland
Great Britain	[ˌgreɪt 'brɪtən]	Großbritannien
Greece	[griːs]	Griechenland
Greek	[griːk]	griechisch
Hanover	['hænəʊvə]	Hannover
Hawaiian	[hə'waɪjən]	hawaiisch
Heathrow	[ˌhiːθ'rəʊ]	*Flughafen im Westen Londons*
Iceland	['aɪslənd]	Island
India	['ɪndiə]	Indien
Indian	['ɪndiən]	indisch
Ireland	['aɪələnd]	Irland
Irish	['aɪərɪʃ]	irisch

Istanbul [ˌɪstæn'bʊːl] Istanbul

Italian [ɪ'tæljən] italienisch

Italy ['ɪtəli] Italien

Jamaica [dʒə'meɪkə] Jamaika

Japan [dʒə'pæn] Japan

Japanese [ˌdʒæpə'niːz] japanisch

Kent ['kent] *Grafschaft südöstlich von London*

Las Vegas [ˌlæs'veɪgəs] Las Vegas

Lisbon ['lɪzbən] Lissabon

London ['lʌndən] London

Luxembourg ['lʌksəmbɜːg] Luxemburg

Mauritius [mə'rɪʃəs] *Inselstaat im Südwesten des Indischen Ozeans*

Melbourne ['melbən] *Hauptstadt des Staates Victoria in Australien*

Mexican ['meksɪkən] mexikanisch

Moscow ['mɒskəʊ] Moskau

Munich ['mjuːnɪk] München

(the) Netherlands ['neðələndz] die Niederlande

New Zealand [ˌnjuː 'ziːlənd] Neuseeland

Newark ['njuːək] *Stadt in New Jersey, USA*

Nuremberg ['njʊərəmˌbɜːg] Nürnberg

Paddington Station [ˌpædɪŋtən 'steɪʃn] *Londoner Bahnhof*

Paris ['pærɪs] Paris

Poland ['pəʊlənd] Polen

Polish ['pəʊlɪʃ] polnisch

Portugal ['pɔːtʃʊgl] Portugal

Prague [prɑːg] Prag

(the) Pyrenees [pɪrə'niːz] (die) Pyrenäen

(the river) Rhine [raɪn] Rhein

Rome [rəʊm] Rom

Russia ['rʌʃə] Russland

Russian ['rʌʃn] russisch

Scotland ['skɒtlənd] Schottland

Scottish ['skɒtɪʃ] schottisch

Siberia [saɪ'bɪəriə] Sibirien

Singapore [ˌsɪŋgə'pɔː] Singapur

South America [ˌsaʊθ ə'merɪkə] Südamerika

Spain [speɪn] Spanien

Spanish ['spænɪʃ] spanisch

Switzerland ['swɪtsələnd] (die) Schweiz

Taj Mahal [ˌtɑːdʒ mə'hɑːl] *indisches Denkmal*

Thai [taɪ] thailändisch, Thai(-)

Thailand ['taɪlænd] Thailand

Tunisia [tju'nɪziə] Tunesien

Turkey ['tɜːki] Türkei

UK [ˌjuː 'keɪ] Vereinigtes Königreich

(the) USA, US [ˌjuː es 'eɪ, ˌjuː 'es] Vereinigte Staaten von Amerika

Vienna [vi'enə] Wien

Wales [weɪlz] Wales

Washington State ['wɒʃɪŋtən ˌsteɪt] *Bundesland im Nordwesten der USA*

Zurich ['zjʊərɪk] Zürich

Irregular Verbs

Infinitive	Past Simple	German
babysit	babysat	babysitten
be	was/were	sein
begin	began	beginnen
bet	bet	wetten
bring	brought	bringen
build	built	bauen
buy	bought	kaufen
can	could	können
choose	chose	wählen, auswählen
come	came	kommen
cost	cost	kosten
dive	dived *(BE)*/dove *(AE)*	tauchen
do	did	tun, machen
drink	drank	trinken
drive	drove	(Auto) fahren
eat	ate	essen
feed	fed	füttern
feel	felt	(sich) fühlen
find	found	finden
fly	flew	fliegen
forget	forgot	vergessen
get	got	bekommen, erlangen; werden
give	gave	geben
go	went	gehen, fahren
grow up	grew up	aufwachsen
have	had	haben
hear	heard	hören
keep	kept	behalten
know	knew	kennen, wissen
lead	led	führen
learn	learned/learnt	sein
leave	left	verlassen; weggehen
let	let	lassen
lie	lay	liegen
lose	lost	verlieren
make	made	machen, anfertigen
mean	meant	bedeuten
meet	met	(sich) treffen; kennen lernen
pay	paid	bezahlen
read [ri:d]	read [red]	lesen
ride	rode	reiten, fahren
ring	rang	anrufen, läuten
run	ran	rennen, laufen

say	**said**	sagen
see	**saw**	sehen
sell	**sold**	verkaufen
send	**sent**	senden, schicken
sing	**sang**	singen
sit	**sat**	sitzen
sleep	**slept**	schlafen
speak	**spoke**	sprechen
spell	**spelled/spelt**	buchstabieren
spend	**spent**	verbringen; ausgeben
stand	**stood**	stehen
steal	**stole**	stehlen
take	**took**	dauern; nehmen
teach	**taught**	unterrichten
tell	**told**	erzählen
think	**thought**	denken; meinen
throw	**threw**	werfen
understand	**understood**	verstehen
wear	**wore**	(Kleidung) tragen
win	**won**	gewinnen
write	**wrote**	schreiben

Numbers

0	zero	**7**	seven	**14**	fourteen
1	one	**8**	eight	**15**	fifteen
2	two	**9**	nine	**16**	sixteen
3	three	**10**	ten	**17**	seventeen
4	four	**11**	eleven	**18**	eighteen
5	five	**12**	twelve	**19**	nineteen
6	six	**13**	thirteen	**20**	twenty

21	twenty-one	**25**	twenty-five	**29**	twenty-nine
22	twenty-two	**26**	twenty-six	**30**	thirty
23	twenty-three	**27**	twenty-seven	**31**	thirty-one
24	twenty-four	**28**	twenty-eight	**32**	thirty-two

40	forty	**100**	a/one hundred
50	fifty	**101**	a/one hundred and one
60	sixty		
70	seventy	**1 000**	a/one thousand
80	eighty	**10 000**	ten thousand
90	ninety	**1 000 000**	a/one million

Alphabetical Register

F = Focus
M = Magazine
QC = Quick Check
S = Story
U = Unit

A, a

a.m. (ante meridiem) von Mitternacht bis Mittag *U5, F2*
ability Fähigkeit *U6, F2*
about über *U1, F1;* (to) **get about** herumkommen *U7, F1*
above oben *U10, F1*
abroad: (to) **go abroad** ins Ausland gehen/fahren *U9, F2*
accommodation Unterkunft *U8, F2*
according to gemäß, nach *U8, F1*
(to) **act out** (etwas) vorspielen *U2, F1*
action Handlung; Aktion *U5, M*
activity Aktivität, Beschäftigung *U6, F2;* **activity holiday** Aktivurlaub *U4, S*
actor Schauspieler *U2, M*
actress Schauspielerin *U2, M*
actually eigentlich, tatsächlich *U6, F2*
adapter Adapter *U11, F1*
(to) **add** hinzufügen *U9, F2*
(to) **add up** zusammenzählen *U10, M*
address Adresse *U2, F2*
(to) **admit** zugeben *U10, S*
(to) **adopt** adoptieren *U6, F2*
adult Erwachsene/r *U6, F2;* **adult education** Erwachsenenbildung *U6, F2*
adventure Abenteuer *U12, F2*
affair: (to) **have an affair** ein Verhältnis haben *U10, S*
afraid: I'm afraid ... leider *U8, F1*
after nach *U5, S;* **after that** danach *U5, M*
afternoon Nachmittag, Nachmittags- *U5, F2*
again wieder, noch einmal *U1, F2*
age Alter *U6, F2;* **age group** Altersgruppe *U6, F2*
agent Vertreter/in *U10, S*
ago vor *U7, F1;* **a long time ago** vor langer Zeit *U7, F2*
(to) **agree** vereinbaren *U7, F2*
air Luft *U6, M;* **airline** Fluggesellschaft *U3, F2;* **airport** Flughafen *U1, F2*
alarm clock Wecker *U5, M*
all alle *U3, F2;* **all over (the country)** überall (im Land) *U8, F1;* **all year round** das ganze Jahr über *U6, F2*
allergic: (to) be allergic to sth gegen etwas allergisch sein *QC3*
all right: It's all right. Ist schon in Ordnung/gut. *U10, F2*
almost fast, beinahe *U3, F2*
alone allein(e) *U8, M*
along entlang *U8, M*
already schon *U7, F1*
also auch *U2, F2*
alternative alternativ *U4, S*
always immer *U3, M*
and und *U1, F1*
angry verärgert, wütend *U5, S*
animal Tier *U3, F2*
another ein/e andere/r/s *U1, F2*
answer Antwort, Lösung *U1, F2*
(to) **answer** antworten *U1, F3*
any irgendwelche, etwas *U9, F2;* **not any** kein/e *U9, M;* **anyone** irgend-jemand *U9, M;* **anything** etwas *U4, F2;* **anything else?** noch etwas? *U4, F2;* **anything like that** etwas dergleichen *U9, M;* **anywhere** irgendwo *U9, M*
apartment *(AE)* Wohnung *U8, M*
April April *U8, F1*
are bist, sind, seid *U1, F1*
argument Auseinandersetzung, Streit *U8, S*
arm Arm *U11, M*
armchair Sessel *QC3*
(to) **arrange** abmachen, vereinbaren *U10, F2*
arrangement Vereinbarung *U12, F2;* (to) **make an arrangement** eine Vereinbarung treffen *U12, F2*
(to) **arrive** ankommen, eintreffen *U2, S*
art Kunst *U10, M;* **art gallery** Kunstgalerie *U9, F1*
article Artikel *U5, S*
as: as much as so viel wie *U4, F2;* **as soon as** sobald *U10, M*

(to) **ask** fragen *U1, F3;* (to) **ask for help** um Hilfe bitten *U12, F3;* (to) **ask the way** nach dem Weg fragen *U11, F3*
at: at home zu Hause *U5, F1;* **at least** zumindest *U5, F2;* **at night** nachts *U3, M;* **at the beginning** am Anfang *U12, F1;* **at the moment** im Moment *U11, M;* **at the same time** gleichzeitig *U6, M*
athletic sportlich *U8, F1*
(to) **attach** anbringen *U2, M*
attention Aufmerksamkeit *U10, M*
attractive attraktiv, anziehend *U4, M*
August August *U8, F1*
aunt Tante *U3, M*
automatic automatisch *U8, M*
autumn Herbst *U10, F1*
avalailable: (to) **be available** (am Telefon) zu sprechen sein *QC3*
away: (to) **be away** weg/unterwegs sein *U1, S*
awful furchtbar, fürchterlich *QC2*

B, b

(to) **babysit** babysitten *U12, F2*
back Rücken *U8, M*
back zurück *U5, F3;* (to) **get back home** wieder nach Hause kommen *U5, M;* (to) **go back** zurückgehen *U5, M*
backpack Rucksack *U11, M*
bad schlecht *U1, F1;* **bad news** schlechte Nachrichten *U10, S*
bag Tasche *U8, F2*
baggage hall Gepäckhalle *U4, S;* **baggage reclaim** Gepäckausgabe *U10, F3*
baked camembert gebackener Camembert *U4, M*
banana Banane *U4, F1*
band Band *U2, S*
bank Bank *U3, F2;* **bank holiday** Feiertag *U6, F2*
barbecue Grillparty *U8, F2;* (to) **have a barbecue** grillen *U8, F2*
basement Untergeschoss *U7, S*
basic wesentlich *U12, F3*
bathroom Bad *U5, M*
battery Batterie *U11, F1*
battle Kampf, Schlacht *U8, F1*
BC *Abk. von* before Christ, vor Christus *U7, M*
(to) **be** sein *U1, M;* (to) **be free** Zeit haben *U12, F2;* (to) **be lucky** Glück haben *U10, F1;* (to) **be missing** fehlen, verschwunden sein *U8, F2;* (to) **be unlucky** Pech haben *U10, F1*
beach Strand *U8, F2*
bean Bohne *U9, F1*
beautiful (wunder)schön *U3, F2*
because weil *U2, S;* **because of** wegen, aufgrund von *U1, S*
bed Bett *U5, F2;* (to) **go to bed** ins Bett gehen *U5, F2*
beer Bier *U4, F1*
before bevor *U2, S;* vor *U5, F2*
beginner Anfänger/in *U6, M*
beginning Anfang *U12, F1;* **at the beginning** am Anfang *U12, F1*
(to) **believe** glauben *U9, M*
below unten *U2, F1*
best beste/r/s *U3, M*
bet wetten *QC2;* **You bet!** Und ob! *QC2*
better besser *U8, F1*
between zwischen *U5, F2*
big groß *U3, F2*
bike: by bike mit dem Rad *U7, F1*
bill Rechnung *U4, F2*
birthday Geburtstag *U1, F3*
bit: a bit ein bisschen *U11, M*
black schwarz *U10, M*
blue blau *U10, M*
board Tafel *U3, F2*
boarding card Bordkarte *U4, F2*
boat Boot, Schiff *U9, F1*
book Buch *U1, M*
(to) **book** buchen, vorbestellen, reservieren *QC3*
(to) **borrow** (sich etwas) ausleihen *U3, M*
born: (to) **be born** geboren sein *U1, F1*
boss Chef/in *U3, F1*
botanic garden botanischer Garten *U6, F2*
both beide *U10, F1*
bottle Flasche *U2, S*
bottom Boden *U11, M*
box Schachtel *U8, M*
boy Junge *U3, F2;* **boyfriend** Freund *U6, M*
brackets Klammern *QC3*
break Pause *U5, F2*

breakfast Frühstück *U5, F1;* (to) **have/eat breakfast** frühstücken *U5, F1;* **for breakfast** zum Frühstück *U5, F1;* **breakfast time** Frühstückszeit *U6, F1*
(to) **breathe down the phone** ins Telefon hauchen *U12, S*
bridge Brücke *U9, F2*
bright hell, kräftig *(Farbe) U11, M*
brochure Broschüre *U6, M*
brother Bruder *U3, F2;* **brother-in-law** Schwager *U3, M*
brown braun *U10, M*
brunch Brunch *U6, F1*
brush Bürste *U11, F1*
brush: (to) **brush your teeth** *(BE)* sich die Zähne putzen *U5, M*
bubble (Sprech-)Blase *U10, F3*
buffet Büfett *U4, F2*
(to) **build** bauen *U8, M*
building Gebäude *U6, F2*
bus (Linien-)Bus *U1, S;* **by bus** mit dem Bus *U7, F1;* **bus lane** Busspur *U7, M;* **bus shelter** Bushäuschen *U7, M;* **bus stop** Bushaltestelle *U7, F2*
business Geschäft, Firma *U1, S;* **on business** dienstlich, geschäftlich *U1, S* **business partner** Geschäftspartner/in *U10, F2;* **business trip** Geschäftsreise *U4, F2*
busy beschäftigt *U6, M*
but aber *U1, F1*
butter Butter *U3, M*
buy kaufen *U2, S*
by: by mistake aus Versehen *U12, S;* **by the sea** am Meer *U8, F2;* **by the way** übrigens *U1, M*
bye Tschüss *U1, S*

C, c

cabin Kabine *U7, M*
café Café, Bistro *U1, F1*
cake Kuchen *U6, F1*
calendar Kalender *U8, F1*
call Anruf, Telefongespräch *U6, F2*
(to) **call** anrufen *U10, F2*
called namens, genannt *U1, F1*
calm ruhig, gelassen *U10, F1*
camel Kamel *U7, M*
camera Fotoapparat, Kamera *U11, F1*
camping Zelten, Camping *U8, F2*
can Dose *U11, F2*
can können *U1, F2*
canal trip Kanalfahrt *U8, M*
can't *verneinte Form von* can, nicht können *U2, S*
canteen Kantine *U3, M*
car Auto *U4, M;* **by car** mit dem Auto *U7, F1*
caravan Wohnwagen *U8, F2*
card Visitenkarte *U4, F2*
cardboard box Pappschachtel *U8, S*
cards Karten *U3, M*
career Karriere *U7, F1*
careful vorsichtig *U10, M*
carefully sorgfältig *U9, M*
carriage Wagen (eines Zuges) *U7, M*
(to) **carry** tragen *U8, F1*
cart Kutsche *U6, F2*
cartoon Cartoon *U1, F2*
case Koffer *U4, S*
cash: in cash in bar *U11, M*
castle Burg, Schloss *U6, F2*
cat Katze *U5, M*
category Kategorie *U6, M*
cathedral Dom, Kathedrale *U9, F2*
(to) **celebrate** feiern *U2, S*
celebration Feier *U8, F1*
cellphone *(AE)* Handy *U1, F3*
central zentral, Zentral- *U11, F3*
centre Zentrum *U3, M*
century Jahrhundert *U8, F1*
ceremony Zeremonie *U9, F1*
chain Kette *U12, M;* **chain store** Filiale (einer Kette) *U11, M*
champagne Champagner *U2, S*
championship Meisterschaft *U8, F1*
changing room Umkleideraum, -kabine *U11, M*
chapel Kapelle *U9, F1*
character Person *U10, F1*
charming charmant, reizend *U10, M*
chat Unterhaltung, Gespräch *U5, F2;* **chat show** *(BE)* Talkshow *U1, F2*
cheap billig, günstig *U9, F1*
(to) **check** überprüfen *U2, F1*
check-in Abfertigung(sschalter) *U1, F3;* **check-in date** Ankunftsdatum *U2, F2;* **check-in desk** Abfertigungsschalter *U7, M*
check-out date Abreisedatum *U2, F2*
cheese Käse *U4, F1*
chef Küchenchef *U3, F1*

chicken Huhn, Hähnchen *U4, M;* **chicken wings** Hähnchenflügel *U4, M*
child, children Kind, Kinder *U3, F2;* (to) **have children** Kinder kriegen *U9, F2*
chips Pommes frites *U4, M*
chocolate Schokolade *U3, M*
choice Auswahl *U9, F1*
(to) **choose** wählen, auswählen *U2, F1*
church Kirche *U6, F1*
cinema Kino *U6, F1*
(to) **circle** einkreisen *U2, F2*
city (Groß)-Stadt *U5, F2;* **city centre** Stadtzentrum *U6, F2*
class Klasse, Kurs *U1, F1*
classical music klassische Musik *U10, F1*
(to) **clean** putzen, reinigen *U7, F2;* (to) **clean your teeth** *(AE)* sich die Zähne putzen *U5, M*
client Kunde/Kundin *U12, F3*
cliff Klippe, Felsen *U8, M*
clock Uhr *U5, F2*
(to) **close** (ver)schließen *U3, F2*
closed geschlossen, gesperrt *U7, F2*
closing time Ende der Öffnungszeit *U6, F2*
cloth Tuch, Stoff *U11, M*
clothes Kleider, Kleidung *U10, F1*
club Klub, Verein *U9, F2*
coffee Kaffee *U2, M;* (to) **make coffee** Kaffee kochen *U5, M;* **coffee machine** Kaffeemaschine *U5, M*
cold kalt *U9, F1*
colleague Kollege/Kollegin *U3, F1*
(to) **collect** sammeln *U9, F2;* abholen *U4, S*
colour *(BE)* Farbe *U10, M*
coloured *(BE)* farbig *U11, M*
column Spalte *U6, F1*
comb Kamm *U11, F1*
combination Kombination, Verbindung *U6, F1*
(to) **come** kommen *U3, S;* (to) **come from ...** aus ... kommen *U3, F2;* (to) **come in** vorbeischauen *U8, F1;* (to) **come out of** herauskommen *U7, F2;* (to) **come to a stop** zum Halten kommen *U8, M*
comfortable bequem *U11, M*
common: (to) have (sth) in common etwas gemeinsam haben *U10, F1*
compact kompakt *U11, F2*
company Unternehmen, Firma *U1, S*
(to) **compare** vergleichen *U4, F1*
comparison Vergleich *U9, F1*
(to) **complete** vervollständigen *U1, F1*
computer expert Computerexperte/-expertin *U1, F1;* **computer game** Computerspiel *U6, F1;* **computer system** Computersystem *U12, F2*
computing EDV *U6, M*
conflict Konflikt *U7, S*
(to) **confront** konfrontieren *U10, S*
contact Kontakt, Begegnung *U1, F1;* **contact address** Kontaktadresse *U2, M*
conversation Gespräch, Unterhaltung *U2, F2*
cook Koch/Köchin *U6, M*
(to) **cook** kochen *U6, F1*
cookie Plätzchen, Keks *U4, M*
cooking Kochen *U6, M*
cooperation Zusammenarbeit *U10, S*
correct richtig *U3, F1*
(to) **cost** kosten *U11, F2*
could könnte/n *U6, F1;* **couldn't** *verneinte Form von* could *U9, M*
country Land, Staat *U2, M*
countryside Landschaft *U8, F2*
county council Bezirksverwaltung *U6, F2*
course Kurs, Lehrgang *U2, M*
cousin Cousin/e *U3, M*
cow Kuh *U7, F1*
(to) **crash** aufprallen, zusammenstoßen *U8, M*
creative kreativ, schöpferisch *U6, M*
creativity Kreativität *U6, M*
credit card Kreditkarte *U2, F2*
cross Kreuz *U5, M;* **cross-country** Langlauf- *U8, F2*
cup Tasse *U5, F2*
curry Curry *U4, F1*
customer Kunde/Kundin *U4, M*
customs Zoll *U10, F3*
cycle rickshaw Fahrradrikscha *U7, M*

D, d
daily täglich *U5, F1*
damn! verdammt! *U1, S*
dance class Tanzunterricht *U6, F2*

dark dunkel *U10, M*
darling Liebling, Schatz *U1, F3*
date Datum *U2, M;* Verabredung *U7, F2;* (to) **have a date** (privat) mit jdm verabredet sein *U7, F2;* **date of birth** Geburtsdatum *U2, F2*
daughter Tochter *U3, F2;* **daughter-in-law** Schwiegertochter *U3, M*
day Tag *U2, M;* **daytime** tagsüber *U8, M*
dear liebe/r *U8, M*
December Dezember *U8, F1*
(to) **decide** entscheiden *U5, F2*
decision Entscheidung *U11, F3;* (to) **make a decision** eine Entscheidung treffen *U10, M*
(to) **declare** verzollen *U10, F3*
definitely bestimmt, sicher(lich) *U6, F1*
deli Delikatessengeschäft *U11, M*
delicious köstlich *U1, M*
dentist Zahnarzt, Zahnärztin *U12, F2*
department store Kauf-, Warenhaus *U11, M*
departure lounge Abflughalle, Warteraum *U7, M*
(to) **describe** beschreiben *U10, F1*
description Beschreibung *U8, F2*
desk (Schreib-)Tisch *U2, F2*
dessert Nachspeise *U4, F1*
destination Reise-, Fahrtziel *U8, F2*
detail Angabe *U2, F2*
(to) **dial** wählen *U10, F2*
dialogue Dialog *U1, F1*
dictionary Wörterbuch *U7, M*
(to) **die** sterben *U9, F2*
diet Diät *U12, QC3*
different verschieden, unterschiedlich *U2, F2*
difficult schwer, schwierig *U3, S*
dinner: (to) **go out for dinner** im Restaurant zu Abend essen *U4, M*
dinner time Abendessenszeit *U6, F1*
direction Richtung, Weg *U11, F3;* (to) **give sb directions** jdm den Weg beschreiben *U11, F3*
(to) **discuss** besprechen, diskutieren *U8, F2*
(to) **dive** tauchen *U6, M*
(to) **divide** teilen *U9, F2*
divorced: (to) **get divorced** sich scheiden lassen *U9, F2*
(to) **do** tun, machen *U1, M;* (to) **do nothing** nichts tun *U8, F2*
doctor Arzt/Ärztin *U1, M*
dog Hund *U3, M*
door Tür *U7, S*
dot Punkt *U2, F2*
double room Doppelzimmer *U2, F1;* **double-decker** Doppeldeckerbus *U7, M*
downstairs (nach) unten *U7, S*
dramatic dramatisch *U12, S*
dressed: (to) **get dressed** (sich) anziehen *U5, M*
drink Getränk *U1, F2;* (to) **go for a drink** einen trinken gehen *U7, F2*
(to) **drink** trinken *U4, F2*
drive (Auto) fahren *U4, M*
driver Fahrer/in *U1, F1*
(to) **drop** fallen lassen *U4, F2*
during während *U10, M*
duty-free shop Duty-free-Shop *U7, M*

E, e

each other einander, gegenseitig *U4, F2*
early früh *U1, M*
ears Ohren *U12, QC3*
east Osten *U9, F2*
easy leicht *U11, M;* **easy-going** unkompliziert *U10, F1*
(to) **eat** essen *U3, M;* (to) **have sth to eat** etwas essen *U4, F2;* (to) **eat out** im Restaurant essen *U4, F2*
editor Redakteur/in *U7, F1*
education Erziehung, Bildung *U6, F2*
eighth achte/r/s *U8, F1*
eleventh elfte/r/s *U8, F1*
email E-Mail *U2, F2*
end: in the end zum Schluss, schließlich *U11, M*
(to) **end** enden *U8, M*
ending Ende *U4, F2*
English Engländer/in *U1, F1;* **in English** auf Englisch *U1, F2*
(to) **enjoy** genießen *U4, M*
enough ausreichend, genug *U7, F2*
entertainment Unterhaltung *U1, F2*
entrance Eingang, Einfahrt *U6, F2*
(to) **escalate** eskalieren *U7, S*
euro Euro *U4, F2*
evening Abend *U2, S;* **evening dress** Abendkleid *U11, F1*
event Ereignis, Veranstaltung *U6, F2*

ever jemals, überhaupt *U6, M*
every jede/r/s *U3, M;* **everyone** jede/r/s *U8, F1;* **everything** alles *U6, S*
ex-wife Ex-Frau *U3, F2*
exactly genau *U9, F2*
example Beispiel *U4, F2;* **for example** zum Beispiel *U3, M*
excellent ausgezeichnet, hervorragend *U6, M*
except außer *U9, F2*
excuse me Entschuldigung. *U5, M*
exercise Übung, Aufgabe *U1, F2*
exp. *Abk. von* expire, ablaufen *U2, F2*
expensive teuer *U4, F2*
expert Experte, Expertin *U1, M*
(to) **explain** erklären *U11, F1*
(to) **explode** explodieren *U3, S*

F, f
fact Tatsache, Fakt *U7, M*
factory Fabrik *U5, F3*
false falsch *U9, F1*
family Familie *U3, F2;* **family name** Familienname *U2, M*
famous berühmt *U3, F2*
fantastic fantastisch *U4, F2*
far weit (entfernt) *U12, F2*
fashion Mode *U1, F2*
fast schnell *U4, M*
father Vater *U1, F1*
favourite liebste/r/s, Lieblings- *U4, F1*
fax Fax *U2, F2*
February Februar *U8, F1*
(to) **feed** füttern *U5, M*
(to) **feel** (sich) fühlen *U10, M;* (to) **feel your best** sich am besten fühlen *U10, M*
female weiblich, Frauen- *U2, M*
festival Festival, Fest(spiele) *U8, F1*
few: a few einige, ein paar *U10, M*
fifteenth fünfzehnte/r/s *U8, F1*
fifth fünfte/r/s *U8, F1*
(to) **fill in** ausfüllen, eintragen *U2, F2*
film *(BE)* Film *U5, M;* **film character** Filmfigur *U4, M*
final letzte/r/s *U5, F3*
(to) **find** finden *U1, F2;* (to) **find out** herausfinden *U1, F3*
fine gut, schön *U1, F1;* **fine arts** schöne Künste *U11, F3*
finger Finger *U6, F2*
(to) **finish** beenden, aufhören *U5, F2*
fireworks Feuerwerk *U8, F1*
first erste/r/s *U1, F1;* **for the first time** zum ersten Mal *U7, M*
first choice erste Wahl *U1, F1;* **first class ticket** Fahrkarte für die erste Klasse *U9, M;* **first name** Vorname *U1, F1*
fish Fisch *U4, F2*
flat *(BE)* Wohnung *U8, F2*
flavour Geschmack, Aroma *U9, F1*
flight Flug *U1, M*
floor Fußboden *U9, F1*
flower Blume *U7, F2*
(to) **fly** fliegen *U7, F2*
(to) **focus on** sich konzentrieren auf *U6, F2*
food Essen, Nahrung(smittel) *U1, F2*
foot, feet Fuß, Füße *U10, M*
football Fußball *U3, F2;* **footballer** Fußballspieler/in *U1, M*
fourteenth vierzehnte/r/s *U8, F1*
fourth vierte/r/s *U8, F1*
free: (to) **be free** Zeit haben *U12, F2*
fresh frisch *U6, M*
Friday Freitag *U6, F1*
friend Freund/in *U3, F2*
friendly freundlich, freundschaftlich *U3, F2*
from von, aus *U1, F1;* (to) **come from ...** aus ... kommen *U3, F2;* **from around the world** aus der ganzen Welt *U4, F1;* **from time to time** von Zeit zu Zeit *U5, F3*
fruit Obst, Früchte *U4, M*
full: (to) **be full of sth** voller ... sein *U7, F2*
funny komisch, lustig *U10, F1*
future Zukunft *U12, F2*

G, g
gallon Gallone *U9, M*
game Spiel *U2, F1*
garden Garten *U3, M*
gardener Gärtner/in *U3, M*
gate Flugsteig *U7, M*
gender Geschlecht *U2, M*
(to) **get** bekommen, erlangen *U6, M;* (to) werden *U8, M;* (to) **get about** herumkommen *U7, F1;* (to) **get back home** wieder nach Hause kommen *U5, M;* (to) **get divorced**

sich scheiden lassen *U9, F2;* (to) **get dressed** (sich) anziehen *U5, M;* (to) **get in** ankommen, landen *QC3;* (to) **get married** heiraten *U9, F2;* (to) **get on (well) with sb** (gut) mit jdm auskommen *U3, S;* (to) **get retrained** eine Umschulung machen *U9, F2;* (to) **get somewhere** irgendwo hinkommen *U7, F1;* (to) **get to the TV studio** im Fernsehstudio ankommen *U5, M;* (to) **get to work** zur Arbeit kommen *U7, F1;* (to) **get up** aufstehen *U3, M*

gig *bei Unterhaltungsmusik:* Konzert, Auftritt *U2, S*

girl Mädchen *U3, F2*

(to) **give** geben *U1, F2;* schenken *U2, S;* (to) **give back** zurückgeben *U7, S;* (to) **give sb directions** jdm den Weg beschreiben *U11, F3*

glass Glas *U5, F2*

glove Handschuh *U11, F1*

(to) **go** gehen, fahren *U2, S;* (to) **go abroad** ins Ausland gehen/fahren *U9, F2;* (to) **go away** wegfahren *U6, S;* (to) **go dancing** tanzen gehen *U6, F1;* (to) **go for a drink** einen trinken gehen *U7, F2;* (to) **go for walks** spazieren gehen, wandern *U8, M;* (to) **go jogging** Joggen *U5, M;* (to) **go out** ausgehen *U4, M;* (to) **go out for dinner** im Restaurant zu Abend essen *U4, M;* (to) **go past sth** an etwas vorbeigehen *U11, M;* (to) **go sightseeing** Sehenswürdigkeiten besuchen *U8, F2;* (to) **go swimming** schwimmen gehen *U6, F1;* (to) **go to bed** ins Bett gehen *U5, F2;* (to) **go to the opera** in die Oper gehen *U12, F2;* (to) **go walking** wandern *U8, F2*

good gut *U2, F1;* **good value** preisgünstig *U11, M;* **good wishes** Glückwünsche *U8, F1*

goodbye auf Wiedersehen *U4, S;* (to) **say goodbye** sich verabschieden *U4, S*

gossip Klatsch, Tratsch *QC3*

granddaughter Enkelin *U3, M;* **grandmother** Großmutter *U3, M;* **grandparents** Großeltern *U3, F2;* **grandson** Enkel *U3, M*

great groß(artig), toll *U1, M*

green grün *U5, S;* **green tourism** alternativer Tourismus *U5, S*

greetings Grüße *U1, M*

grey grau *U10, M*

group Gruppe *U1, F1;* **group profile** Gruppenprofil *U5, F1*

(to) **grow up** aufwachsen *U9, F2*

(to) **guarantee** garantieren *U2, F2*

guess Vermutung *U7, F1*

(to) **guess** (er)raten *U3, F2*

guest Gast *U2, F1*

guide Führer, Ratgeber *U4, F2*

guidebook Reiseführer *U11, F1*

guided walk geführte Wanderung *U6, F2*

gym Sportstudio, Fitnessstudio *U6, F1*

H, h

habit Angewohnheit *U5, F1*

hairdryer Fön *U11, F1*

half past (six) halb (sieben) *U5, F2*

ham Schinken *U4, F2*

hamburger Hamburger *U1, F2*

hand baggage Handgepäck *U4, S;* **hand luggage** Handgepäck *U11, F1*

handball Handball *U9, M*

(to) **happen** passieren, geschehen *U4, F2*

happy glücklich, fröhlich *U1, F3;* (to) **be happy about sth** über etwas erfreut/glücklich sein *U5, S;* **happy hour** Happy Hour *U6, F1*

hard schwer, hart *U5, F3*

hat Hut *U10, F1*

(to) **hate** hassen *U4, F2*

(to) **have** haben *U1, F3;* (to) **have a barbecue** grillen *U8, F2;* (to) **have a date** (privat) mit jdm verabredet sein *U7, F2;* (to) **have a lie-in** ausschlafen *U8, F2;* (to) **have a look at sth** sich etwas anschauen *U11, F2;* (to) **have a meeting** eine Besprechung haben *U1, S;* (to) **have a party** eine Party feiern *U3, M;* (to) **have a rest** sich ausruhen *U7, F1;* (to) **have a shower** *(BE)* (sich) duschen *U5, M;* (to) **have an affair** ein Verhältnis haben *U10, S;* (to) **have children** Kinder kriegen *U9, F2;* (to) **have sth to eat** etwas essen *U4, F2;* (to) **have/eat breakfast** frühstücken *U5, F1;* (to) **have/eat**

lunch zu Mittag essen *U5, F1*
(to) **have to** müssen *U5, F3*
he er *U1, F1*
head up mit erhobenem Kopf; Kopf hoch *U10, M*
heading Überschrift *U8, F2*
health-food shop Naturkostladen *U11, F2*
(to) **hear** hören *U1, F3;* (to) **hear a rumour** ein Gerücht hören *U9, S*
heavy schwer (Gewicht) *U12, QC3*
hello hallo *U1, F1;* (to) **say hello to sb** jdn begrüßen *U1, F1*
help Hilfe *U12, F2;* (to) **ask for help** um Hilfe bitten *U12, F3*
(to) **help** helfen *U2, F1*
her ihr *U1, F1*
here hier *U1, M*
high hoch *U9, F1*
(to) **highlight** hervorheben, unterstreichen *U6, F2*
him ihn, ihm *U5, F2*
himself sich (selbst), er selbst *U11, M*
his sein *U1, F1*
historic building historisches Gebäude *U9, F2*
history Geschichte *U7, M*
hobby Hobby *U1, F1*
holiday Ferien, Urlaub *U3, M;* (to) **be on holiday** im Urlaub sein *U3, M;* (to) **go on holiday** in den Urlaub fahren *U8, F2*
home zu Hause *U2, S;* **at home** zu Hause *U5, F1*
hometown Heimatort *U9, F2;*
homework Hausaufgaben *U5, F3*
(to) **hope** hoffen *U10, M*
horse Pferd *U6, F2*
hot heiß *U8, F2*
hotel Hotel *U1, F1*
house Haus *U1, F3;* **house number** Hausnummer *U1, F3*
how wie *U1, F1;* **how many** wie viele *U1, F2;* **how much** wie viel *U4, F2*
however doch, jedoch *U9, F1*
hungry hungrig *U4, F2*
husband Ehemann *U3, F2*
hyphen minus *U2, F2*

I, i
I ich *U1, F1*
ice cream parlour Eisdiele *U9, F1*
idea Idee, Gedanke *U6, M*
ideal ideal *U3, M*
identity card Personalausweis *U2, M;* **identity card number** Ausweisnummer *U2, M*
if wenn, falls *U2, F2*
ill *(BE)* krank *U8, F1*
illegal rechtswidrig, illegal *U8, F1*
immediately unverzüglich *U10, F3*
important wichtig *U8, F1*
impulsive impulsiv *U10, M*
indoor Innen-, Hallen- *U6, F2*
information Information(en) *U2, F2*
inline-skating Inlineskaten *U6, F1*
inside innen, Innen(-) *U9, F1*
interested: (to) **be interested in sth** an etwas interessiert sein *U5, S*
interesting interessant *U3, F2*
international international *U1, F1*
interview Interview *U4, F2*
(to) **interview** befragen, interviewen *U5, F1*
intonation Tonfall *U11, F3*
(to) **introduce (oneself)** (sich) vorstellen *U2, F1*
(to) **invite** einladen *U3, M*
irregular unregelmäßig *U7, F2*
island Insel *U10, F1*
IT *Abk. von* information technology, IT *U12, F2*
it es *U1, F3;* **isn't it?** nicht wahr? *U3, F2*
item Ding, Gegenstand *U1, F2*
its sein/e, ihr/e *U2, S*

J, j
jacket Jacke, Jackett *U7, F2*
January Januar *U8, F1*
job Arbeit, Beruf *U1, F1*
jogging: (to) **go jogging** joggen *U5, M*
journalist Journalist/in *U1, F1*
July Juli *U8, F1*
June Juni *U8, F1*
just (ganz) einfach *U3, S;* nur *U4, F2;* lediglich *U7, S*

K, k
karaoke Karaoke *U1, F1*
(to) **keep** bleiben *U2, F1;* behalten *U11, F2*
key Schlüssel *U9, M*
kilometre Kilometer *U5, F3*

kind freundlich, nett *U11, F3*
kitchen Küche *U5, M*
kiwi Kiwi *U4, F1*
(to) **know** kennen *U3, F2*

L, l
lake See *U6, M*
landscape Landschaft *U6, M;* **landscape gardening** Landschaftsgärtnerei *U6, M*
language Sprache *U6, F2*
large groß *U4, F2*
last letzte/r/ *U3, F2;* zuletzt, das letzte Mal *U7, F2*
late spät *U1, S;* (to) **be late** (zu) spät kommen *U1, S*
later später *U1, M*
(to) **laze about** herumfaulenzen *QC2*
(to) **lead** führen *U9, F2*
leaflet Faltblatt *U6, F2*
(to) **learn** lernen *U6, F2*
least: at least zumindest, mindestens *U5, F2*
(to) **leave** weggehen; verlassen *U2, S;* (to) **leave school** von der Schule abgehen *U9, F2*
left übrig *U7, F2*
legal rechtmäßig, legal *U8, F1*
leisure Freizeit *U6, F2*
lemon juice Zitronensaft *U11, M*
lesson Unterrichtsstunde *U11, F2*
(to) **let** lassen *U10, F3*
letter Buchstabe *U2, F2*
lie-in: (to) **have a lie-in** ausschlafen *U8, F2*
(to) **lie** liegen *U8, F2;* (to) **lie on the beach** am Strand liegen *U8, F2*
life Leben *U3, F1;* **life history** Lebensgeschichte *U9, F2*
lift Aufzug, Fahrstuhl *U7, F2*
light hell *U10, M*
like wie *U3, M*
(to) **like** mögen, gern haben *U3, F2*
line (Telefon-)Leitung *U10, F2;* **(in) line** (in der) Reihe *U8, F1*
list Liste *U1, F2*
(to) **listen (to)** zuhören, anhören *U1, F1*
litre (of sth) Liter *U3, M*
(to) **live** wohnen, leben *U3, F2*
lively lebendig, lebhaft *U10, F1*
live music Livemusik *U4, F2*
lobster Hummer *U8, M*
local lokal, einheimisch *U10, S*
long lang *U5, F2;* **for long** lange *U7, F2;* **long-distance walking** Wandern *U10, F1*
look: (to) **have a look at sth** sich etwas anschauen *U11, F2*
(to) **look ahead** vorausschauen *U12, F1;* (to) **look at** ansehen, betrachten *U1, F1;* (to) **look back** zurückblicken *U12, F1;* (to) **look for sth** (nach) etwas suchen *U11, F2;* (to) **look like** aussehen wie *U3, M;* (to) **look round** sich umsehen *U2, F1*
Lord of the Rings Herr der Ringe *(Buchtitel) U10, F1*
(to) **lose** verlieren *U7, F2*
lot: a lot of viel, viele *U5, F1*
lots of viel, viele *U3, M*
loud laut *U10, M;* **loud entrance** lauter Auftritt *U10, M*
(to) **love** lieben, gern mögen *U4, F2*
lovely schön, herrlich *U8, F1*
lucky: (to) **be lucky** Glück haben *U10, F1*
luggage Gepäck *U11, F1*
lunch Mittagessen *U5, F1;* (to) **have/eat lunch** zu Mittag essen *U5, F1;* **lunchtime** Mittagszeit *U6, F1*
luxury Luxus *U8, F2*

M, m
magazine Magazin, Zeitschrift *U1, F1*
mail *Abk. von* email, Mail *U2, F2*
main course Hauptgericht *U4, M;* **main meal** Hauptmahlzeit *U5, F1;* **main road** Hauptstraße *U9, M*
(to) **make** machen, anfertigen *U1, F2;* (to) **make a decision** eine Entscheidung treffen *U10, M;* (to) **make an arrangement** eine Vereinbarung treffen *U12, F2;* (to) **make coffee** Kaffee kochen *U5, M;* (to) **make printouts** ausdrucken *U8, S*
male männlich, Männer- *U2, M*
man, men Mann, Männer *U8, F1*
map Stadtplan *U11, F1*
March März *U8, F1*
(to) **march** marschieren *U8, S*
market Markt *U4, F2*
married: (to) **be married** verheiratet

N, n

never nie(mals) *U4, F2*
new neu *U3, F2*
New Year's Eve Silvester *U8, M*
news Nachrichten *U7, F1;* **bad news** schlechte Nachrichten *U10, S*
newspaper Zeitung *U5, M*
next nächste/r/s *U3, S;* **next door** nebenan *U9, M*
nice nett, schön *U1, F1*
niece Nichte *U3, M*
night Nacht *U2, F1;* **at night** nachts *U3, M*
ninth neunte/r/s *U8, F1*
no nein *U1, F3;* kein/e *U7, F2;* **no problem** kein Problem *U1, F3*
nobody niemand *U8, F1*
noisy laut, lärmend *U9, M*
non-smoker Nichtraucher *U2, F1;* **non-smoking** Nichtraucher- *U4, M*
noon Mittag *U5, M*
normal normal *U5, F1*
normally normalerweise *U5, M*
north Nord-, nördlich *U6, F2*
northern Nord-, nördlich *U4, S*
not nicht *U1, F1;* **not any** kein/e *U9, F2;* **not at all** überhaupt nicht *U4, F2*
note Notiz *U4, F2;* (to) **take notes** sich Notizen machen *U5, F1*
nothing nichts *U7, F2*
novel Roman *U11, F1*
November November *U8, F1*
now nun, jetzt *U1, F1;* **nowadays** heutzutage *U9, F2*
number (Telefon-)Nummer *U1, F3;* **a number of** eine Reihe von *U9, S*
(to) **number** nummerieren *U5, M*

O, o

o'clock (um) ... Uhr *U5, F2*
occupation Beruf, Tätigkeit *U2, M*
October Oktober *U8, F1*
odd one out nicht dazugehörig *U1, F2*
of course natürlich, selbstverständlich *U3, M*
offer Angebot *U6, M*
office Büro *U1, M*
often oft, häufig *U1, S*
old alt *U5, F2*
olive Olive *QC3*
Olympics Olympische Spiele *QC2*
once einmal *U6, F1*
one eine/r/s *U2, F2;* **one more time** noch einmal *U8, S*
only nur *U2, F2;* erst *U8, M*
(to) **open** öffnen *U9, M*
open offen, geöffnet *U5, F3*
opera Oper *U12, F2;* (to) **go to the opera** in die Oper gehen *U12, F2*
or oder *U2, F2*
orange orange *U10, M*
order Reihenfolge *U5, M;* (to) **be out of order** außer Betrieb sein *U7, F2*
(to) **order** bestellen *U4, M*
organization Organisation *U9, S*
(to) **organize** organisieren *U4, S*
organized gut organisiert *U10, F1*
other andere/r/s *U1, F1*
our unser *U1, M*
out: (to) **be out all the time** die ganze Zeit unterwegs sein *U6, F2;* (to) **be out and about** unterwegs sein *U11, F1;* (to) **go out** ausgehen *U4, M*
outdoor im Freien *U6, F2*
outside außen, Außen(-) *U9, F1*
over here hier drüben *U4, M;* **over there** da/dort (drüben) *U8, F1;* **over the weekend** übers Wochenende *U12, F2*
own eigene/r/s *U7, F1*
owner Besitzer/in *U1, F1*

P, p

p.m. (post meridiem) von Mittag bis Mitternacht *U5, F2*
(to) **pack** einpacken *U8, F2*
package holiday Pauschalreise *U8, F2*
(to) **paint** malen *U6, M*
painting Malen *U6, F2*
pair Paar *U4, F1*
palace Palast *U11, F3*
paper Zeitung *U10, S;* Papier *U11, F1*
pardon? wie bitte? *U1, F3*
parents Eltern *U3, F2*
park Park *U5, F1*
part Teil *U5, F2*
party Party *U3, M;* (to) **have a party** eine Party feiern *U3, M*
passenger Passagier *U7, F1*
passport (Reise-)Pass *U2, F1;* **passport number** Passnummer *U2, F2*
past nach *U5, F2;* **half past (six)** halb

(sieben) *U5, F2;* **quarter past** Viertel nach *U5, F2;* (to) **go past sth** an etwas vorbeigehen *U11, M*
paté Pastete *QC3*
payment Zahlung *U2, F2*
peanut butter Erdnussbutter *U10, F1*
pen Füller, Kugelschreiber *U11, F1*
people Leute, Menschen *U1, F1*
per day/hour/week pro Tag/Stunde/Woche *U10, F2*
perfect perfekt *U6, M*
perhaps vielleicht, eventuell *U6, F1*
person *Sing. von* people, Mensch, Person *U3, F2*
personal details persönliche Angaben *U2, M*
personality Persönlichkeit *U10, M*
petrol Benzin *U11, F2;* **petrol station** Tankstelle *U11, F2*
phone Telefon *U3, F1;* (to) **be on the phone** am Telefon sein *U3, F1*
(to) **phone** anrufen, telefonieren *U1, S*
phone call Anruf, Telefongespräch *U1, F3*
phone number Telefonnummer *U1, F3*
photo Foto *U1, F1;* **in this photo** auf diesem Foto *U3, M*
photography Fotografie *U6, M*
phrase (Rede-)Wendung *U1, S*
phrasebook *Buch mit Redewendungen* *U11, F1*
(to) **pick up** abholen *U6, F2*
picture Bild *U1, M*
piece Stück *U7, F2*
pilot Pilot/in *U7, M*
pink pink, rosa *U10, M*
pint Pint *U9, M*
pity: That's a pity. Das ist schade. *U10, M*
pizza Pizza *U1, F2*
place Stelle, Platz, Ort *U8, F2*
plan Plan *U8, S*
(to) **plan** planen *U6, S*
plane Flugzeug *U4, F2*
platform Gleis, Bahnsteig *U7, M*
(to) **play** spielen *U3, F2*
playground Spielplatz *U9, M*
please bitte *U2, F1*
pocket Tasche *U10, F3*
point Punkt *U10, M*
police Polizei *U8, M;* **police station** Polizeiwache, -revier *U8, M*
polite höflich *U11, F3*
politician Politiker/in *U2, M*
politics Politik *U7, F2*
pond Teich *U9, F1*
poor arm *U9, F1*
popular beliebt, populär *U4, F2*
portion Portion *U4, M*
position Stellung, Position *U6, F1*
positive bejahend, positiv *U2, F1*
possible möglich, denkbar *U7, F2*
postcard Postkarte *U6, F1;* **post code** Postleitzahl *U2, M;* **post office** Postamt *U11, F3*
poster Plakat *U9, F2*
practical praktisch *U5, F3;* **practical skills** praktische Fähigkeiten *U6, M*
practice session Übungsstunde *U2, S*
(to) **practise** üben *U2, F1*
prawn cocktail Krabbencocktail *U4,M*
(to) **prefer** lieber mögen, bevorzugen *U4, F2*
(to) **prepare** (sich) vorbereiten *U11, F1*
present Geschenk *U9, M*
price (Kauf-)Preis *U11, F2*
private privat *U8, F1*
professional professionell, hauptberuflich *U3, F2*
project Projekt *U10, S*
pub Kneipe *U6, F1*
pullover Pullover *U11, F1*
purple lila *U10, M*

Q, q

quality Qualität *U11, M*
quarter past Viertel nach *U5, F2;* **quarter to** Viertel vor *U5, F2*
question Frage *U2, F1*
quick schnell *U5, F2*
quiet still, ruhig *U8, F1*
quite ziemlich *U4, F2*
quiz Quiz *U4, F1*

R, r

radio Radio *U3, M*
railway Bahn, Eisenbahn *U7, M*
(to) **rain** regnen *U8, F2*
ranch Ranch, Rinderfarm *U1, F1*
(to) **react** reagieren *U10, M*
(to) **read** lesen *U1, F1*
reader Leser/in *U5, S*
ready: (to) **be ready to do sth** bereit sein, etwas zu tun *U4, M*

really wirklich, tatsächlich *U4, F2*
recent aktuell *U2, M*
reception (desk) Rezeption *U2, F2*
recording Aufnahme, Aufzeichnung *U6, F1*
red rot *U7, F2*
registration form Anmeldeformular *U2, M*
regular regelmäßig *U7, F2*
relative Verwandte/r *U8, F2*
(to) **relax** (sich) entspannen *U8, F2*
relaxing erholsam, entspannend *U8, F2*
(to) **remember** sich erinnern (an) *U2, F1*
(to) **repeat** wiederholen *U1, F2*
(to) **report sth to sb** jdm etwas berichten *U5, F1*
reporter Reporter/in *U1, M*
reservation Reservierung *U2, F1*
rest Ruhepause *U7, F1;* (to) **have a rest** sich ausruhen *U7, F1*
restaurant Restaurant *U1, M*
(to) **retell** nacherzählen *U8, F2*
(to) **retire** in den Ruhestand gehen *U9, F2*
retrained: (to) **get retrained** eine Umschulung machen *U9, F2*
rice Reis *U4, M*
rich reich, wohlhabend *U9, F1*
rickshaw Rikscha *U7, M*
ride Fahrt *U6, F2*
(to) **ride** *Fahrrad, Rikscha oder Motorrad* fahren *U7, M*
right richtig *U2, F1;* nicht wahr? *U2, F1;* **right** okay, in Ordnung *U6, F2*
(to) **ring** klingeln *U3, F1*
river Fluss *U9, F2*
road Straße *U11, F3*
roll Brötchen *U4, F2*
roller skates Rollschuhe *U9, F1*
romantic romantisch *U6, S*
rose Rose *U9, F1*
routine Routine, Tagesablauf *U5, F2*
rule Regel *U11, M*
(to) **run** rennen, laufen *U7, F2*

S, s

sad traurig *U10, F1*
(to) **sail** segeln *U6, M*
sailing Segeln *U6, M*
salad Salat *U4, M*
sales manager Verkaufsleiter/in *U4, S*
(the) same der, die, das gleiche *U3, F2*
sandals Sandalen *U11, F1*
sandcastle Sandburg *U8, M*
Saturday Samstag *U6, F1*
sauna Sauna *U6, F1*
(to) **save** sparen *U7, F2*
(to) **say** sagen *U1, F1;* (to) **say good-bye** sich verabschieden *U4, S;* (to) **say hello to sb** jdn begrüßen *U1, F1*
scarf Schal *U11, F1*
schedule Zeitplan *U12, F2*
school Schule *U2, M;* (to) **leave school** von der Schule abgehen *U9, F2;* **schoolbook** Schulbuch *U11, F2;* **schoolchild** Schulkind *U5, F3*
science Wissenschaft *U7, F2*
scissors Schere *U11, F1*
scuba-diving Sporttauchen *(mit Tauchgerät) U6, M*
sea Meer *U8, F2;* **by the sea** am Meer *U8, F2*
season Jahreszeit *U10, F1*
seat Sitz *U9, F1*
second zweite/r/s *U8, F1;* **second class ticket** Fahrkarte für die zweite Klasse *U9, M;* **the second time** das zweite Mal *U3, F1*
secret Geheimnis *U6, M*
security code Sicherheitscode *U2, F2*
(to) **see** sehen *U1, M*
selection Auswahl *U4, F2*
(to) **sell** verkaufen *U6, M*
seminar Seminar, Fachtagung *U9, S*
(to) **send** senden, schicken *U2, F2*
sentence Satz *U1, F3*
September September *U8, F1*
serious ernst(haft) *U10, F1*
(to) **serve** bedienen *U9, F1*
service Bedienung, Service *U4, F2;* **service job** Dienstleistungsberuf *U5, F3*
seventh siebente/r/s *U8, F1*
shall sollen; werden *U6, F2*
shampoo Shampoo *U11, F1*
she sie *U1, F1*
shop Geschäft, Laden *U2, S;* **shop assistant** Verkäufer/in *U11, M*
shopping: (to) **go shopping** einkau-

fen gehen *U5, F2;* **shopping mall** Einkaufszentrum *U11, M*
short form Kurzform *U2, F1*
shorts kurze Hose, Shorts *U1, F2*
should sollte/n, solltest, solltet *U9, F2*
(to) **show** zeigen *U2, F1*
shower Dusche *U5, M;*
(to) **shower** (sich) duschen *U5, M;* (to) **have a shower** *(BE)* (sich) duschen *U5, M;* (to) **take a shower** *(AE)* sich duschen *U5, M*
shy schüchtern *U10, M*
sick *(AE)* krank *U8, F1*
side Seite *U8, F1;* **side dish** Beilage *U4, M;* **side pocket** Seitentasche *U11, M*
sights Sehenswürdigkeiten *U6, F2*
sightseeing: (to) **go sightseeing** Sehenswürdigkeiten besuchen *U8, F2*
signature Unterschrift *U2, M*
silver Silber *U9, F1*
simple einfach *U11, M*
singer Sänger/in *U2, M*
single allein stehend *U1, F1;* **single (room)** Einzelzimmer *U2, F1*
sister Schwester *U3, F2;* **sister-in-law** Schwägerin *U3, M*
(to) **sit** sitzen *U8, F2;* (to) **sit down** sich setzen *U7, S*
situation Situation, Lage *U10, F1*
sixth sechst/r/s *U8, F1*
size Größe *U11, M*
ski Ski *U7, M*
skiing Skilaufen *U8, F2*
skill Fähigkeit, Fertigkeit *U6, M*
(to) **sleep** schlafen *U5, F3*
slogan Slogan, Werbespruch *U9, F2*
slow langsam *U7, F2*
small klein *U4, F2*
(to) **smoke** rauchen *U6, M*
smoker Raucher *U2, F1*
smoking Raucher- *U4, M*
snack Imbiss *U1, F2*
snowboarding Snowboarden *U1, F2*
soap opera Seifenoper *U10, F1*
some einige, etwas *U2, F1;* **someone** jemand *U3, F2;* **something** etwas *U1, F3;* **sometimes** manchmal *U5, F2;* **somewhere** irgendwohin *U7, F2*
son Sohn *U3, F2*
soon bald *U10, S;* **as soon as** sobald *U10, M*
sorry tut mir Leid *U1, F3*
sort: that sort of … solche/derlei … *U5, S*
(to) **sort** sortieren *U7, F2*
(to) **sound** klingen *U9, F2*
sound card Soundkarte *U1, F2*
soup Suppe *QC3*
south Süden *U9, F1*
souvenir Andenken, Souvenir *U8, F2*
spaghetti Spaghetti *U1, F2*
sparkling sprudelnd (Wasser) *QC3*
(to) **speak** sprechen *U3, M;* (to) **speak to sb** mit jdm sprechen *U3, M*
special besondere/r/s, Spezial- *U4, F2*
special offer Sonderangebot *U11, F2*
(to) **spell** buchstabieren *U2, F2*
(to) **spend free time** Freizeit verbringen *U10, F1;* (to) **spend money** Geld ausgeben *U7, F2*
spontaneous spontan *U11, F3*
sport *(BE)* Sport *U1, F1*
spring Frühling *U10, M*
square Platz *U11, F3*
stamp Briefmarke *U11, M*
(to) **stand** stehen *U8, F1*
(to) **start** anfangen, beginnen *U5, F2*
starter Vorspeise *U4, M*
station Bahnhof *U7, F2*
stay Aufenthalt *U8, M*
(to) **stay** bleiben; wohnen *U7, F2*
(to) **steal** stehlen *U8, F1*
still still *(Wasser) U12, QC3*
(to) **stop (at)** halten (an) *U7, F2*
store *(AE)* Geschäft, Warenhaus *U8, M*
story Geschichte *U1, S*
straight direkt *U5, F2;* **straight through** direkt durch *U4, S*
street Straße *U2, M*
stress Betonung *U10, F1*
stressed betont *U6, F1*
stressful anstrengend, stressig *U11, M*
student Schüler/in, Student/in *U2, F1*
studio Studio *U5, M*
stuff *umgangssprachlich:* Zeugs *U12, S*
suddenly plötzlich *U7, F2*
suitcase Koffer *U4, S*
summer Sommer *U5, F3*
(to) **sum up** zusammenfassen *U12, F3*
sun Sonne *U8, F2*

(to) **sunbathe** sonnenbaden *U8, M*
Sunday Sonntag *U5, F3;* **on Sunday** sonntags *U5, F3*
sunglasses Sonnenbrille *U11, F1*
sunny sonnig *U8, M*
sunscreen Sonnenschutzmittel *U11, F1;* **sunshine** Sonnenschein *QC2*
super super, toll *U1, F1*
supermarket Supermarkt *U8, M*
(to) **suppose** annehmen, vermuten *U6, F2*
sure sicher *U3, M;* (to) **be sure** sich sicher sein *U3, M*
(to) **surf the internet** im Internet surfen *U6, F1*
surname Nachname *U1, F1*
surprise Überraschung *U8, M*
survey Umfrage, Übersicht *U11, F2*
sushi *jap. Fischgericht* *U4, F1*
sweatshirt Sweatshirt *U1, F2*
(to) **switch off** ausschalten *U5, M;* (to) **switch on** an-, einschalten *U5, M*
system System *U8, F1*

T, t

table Tabelle *U1, F1*
(to) **take** nehmen *U7, F1;* akzeptieren *U11, M;* (to) **take a shower** *(AE)* sich duschen *U5, M;* (to) **take a taxi** ein Taxi nehmen *U1, S;* (to) **take away** mitnehmen *U4, F2;* (to) **take notes** sich Notizen machen *U5, F1;* (to) **take part in** teilnehmen an *U8, F1;* (to) **take place** stattfinden *U6, F2;* (to) **take sb to …** jdn mitnehmen, irgendwohin bringen *U8, M*
takeover Übernahme, Fusion *U9, S*
talk Gespräch, Unterhaltung *U6, S*
(to) **talk about sth** über etwas sprechen *U3, F2;* **talk show** *(AE)* Talkshow *U1, F2*
talkative redselig, gesprächig *U10, F1*
(to) **taste** *(Speisen)* probieren, versuchen *U6, F2*
tax advisor Steuerberater/in *U12, F2*
taxi Taxi *U1, F1;* **by taxi** mit dem Taxi *U7, F1;* (to) **take a taxi** ein Taxi nehmen *U1, S*
tea Tee *U2, M;* **tea time** Teezeit *U6, F1*
(to) **teach** unterrichten *U5, F3*
teacher Lehrer/in *U1, F1*
team Mannschaft *U1, F2*
teammate Teammitglied *U10, S*
telephone Telefon *U2, F2*
television Fernsehen *U3, M*
(to) **tell sb sth** jdm etwas sagen/erzählen *U1, F1*
temperature Temperatur *U9, F1*
temple Tempel *U9, F1*
tennis player Tennisspieler/in *U3, F2*
tent Zelt *U8, M*
tenth zehnte/r/s *U8, F1*
(to) **test** prüfen, testen *U2, F1*
text (message) SMS *U2, F2*
Thai boxing Thaiboxen *U9, F1*
than als *U9, F1*
thank you, thanks danke *U1, F1*
that dies/e/r *U2, F2*
theatre Theater *U11, F3*
their ihr/e *U3, F2*
them *3. Person Plural:* sie, ihnen *U1, F1*
then dann *U1, F1*
therapist Therapeut/in *U3, F2*
there da, dort *U1, F1;* **there are** es gibt *U7, F1;* **there is** es gibt *U4, F2*
these Pl. von this, diese *U1, F2*
they *3. Person Plural:* sie *U1, F2*
thing Sache, Ding, Gegenstand *U3, M*
(to) **think** glauben, denken, meinen *U2, F1;* (to) **think of sth/sb** sich etw ausdenken, an etwas/jdn denken *U12, F3*
third dritte/r/s *U8, F1*
thirteenth dreizehnte/r/s *U8, F1*
this diese/r/s *U2, F2;* **this is …** dies ist … *U1, F1*
those: two of those zwei davon *U11, M*
thousands of … Tausende … *U8, F1*
through durch *U7, S*
(to) **throw** werfen *U8, F1*
Thursday Donnerstag *U6, F1*
(to) **tick** abhaken, ankreuzen *U1, F3*
(to) **tie** (an)binden *U11, M*
tiger Tiger *U6, F2*
till bis *U5, F3*
time Uhrzeit *U5, F2;* **a long time ago** vor langer Zeit *U7, F2;* **at the same time** gleichzeitig *U6, M;* **from time to time** von Zeit zu Zeit *U5, F3;* (to) **have a good time** sich amüsieren, viel Spaß haben *U7, M;* **for the first time** zum ersten

Mal *U7, M;* **the second time** das zweite Mal *U3, F1;* **one more time** noch einmal *U8, S*
time expressions Zeitangaben *U6, F1;* **timeline** Zeitachse *U8, F2*
times mal *U6, F1*
tired müde *U9, M*
title Titel *U2, M*
today heute *U1, S*
together zusammen *U2, S*
tomato Tomate *U4, F1;* **tomato ketchup** Ketchup *U4, F1*
tomorrow morgen *U7, S*
too auch *U1, F1;* **me too** ich auch *U4, F2;* zu *U5, S*
tool Werkzeug *U3, M*
topic Thema *U7, M*
tour Tour, Reise *U6, F1;* **tour guide** Reiseführer/in *U6, F2*
tourism Tourismus *U5, S;* **green tourism** alternativer Tourismus *U5, S*
tourist Tourist/in *U6, F2*
town Stadt *U2, M;* **town hall** Rathaus *U9, F1*
toy Spielzeug *U11, M*
tradition Brauch, Tradition *U8, F1*
traditional traditionell *U8, F1*
traffic (Straßen-)Verkehr *U7, F2;* **traffic lights** Ampel *U7, F2*
train Zug *U7, F1;* **by train** mit der Bahn *U7, F1*
transport öffentliche Verkehrsmittel, Transport *U7, M*
travel Reisen *U1, F2;* **travel company** Reiseunternehmen *U5, F2;* **travel firm** Reiseveranstalter *U4, S;* **travel magazine** Reisemagazin *U1, F1*
treasure Schatz *U12, M;* **treasure hunt** Schatzsuche *U12, M*
trouble Ärger *U11, M*
true richtig, wahr *U6, F2*
(to) **try** probieren *U4, F2;* (to) **try sth on** etwas anprobieren *U11, F2*
Tuesday Dienstag *U6, F1*
tuk tuk motorisierte Rikscha *U7, M*
tuna Tunfisch *U9, F1*
turquoise türkis *U10, M*
TV presenter Fernsehmoderator/in *U5, M*
twelfth zwölfte/r/s *U8, F1*
twenty-first einundzwanzigste/r/s *U8, F1*
twentysomething jemand in den Zwanzigern *U9, M*
twice zweimal *U6, F1*
type of Art von *U12, F1*
typical typisch *U5, F1*

U, u
umbrella (Regen-)Schirm *U11, F1*
uncle Onkel *U3, M*
under unter *U3, M*
underground U-Bahn *U7, F2;* **by underground** mit der U-Bahn *U7, F1*
(to) **underline** unterstreichen *U12, F2*
underscore Unterstrich *U2, F2*
(to) **understand** verstehen *U12, F3*
university Universität *U9, F2*
(to) **unpack** auspacken *U8, F2*
unlucky: (to) **be unlucky** Pech haben *U10, F1*
untidy unordentlich, unaufgeräumt *U10, F1*
unusual ungewöhnlich *U3, F2;* **unusually** ungewöhnlich(erweise) *U10, S*
us uns *U4, F2*
(to) **use** gebrauchen, benutzen *U10, F2*
usually normalerweise, gewöhnlich *U5, F2*

V, v
vacation *(AE)* Urlaub, Ferien *U11, M*
value Wert *U11, M;* **good value** preisgünstig *U11, M*
vanilla Vanille *U9, F1*
vegetable lasagne Gemüse-Lasagne *U4, M*
vegetarian Vegetarier/in *U4, F2*
verb Verb *U3, F2*
very sehr *U1, S;* **very much** sehr *U3, F2*
video Video(film) *U6, F1*
village Dorf *U7, M*
visit Besuch *U8, M*
(to) **visit** besuchen *U6, F2*
visitor Besucher/in *U6, F2*
vodka Wodka *U4, F1*
voice Stimme *U8, F1*
volleyball Volleyball *U1, F2*

W, w
(to) **wait** warten *U9, S*
waiter Kellner *U4, F2*
waiting room Warteraum *U7, M*
waitress Kellnerin *U4, F2*
walk: (to) **go for walks** spazieren gehen, wandern *U8, M*
(to) **walk** (zu Fuß) gehen *U2, F2*
walking shoes Wanderschuhe *U11, F1*
wall Wand, Mauer *U8, M*
(to) **want** wollen *U7, F2*
war Krieg *U8, M;* **war veteran** Kriegsveteran *U8, M*
warm warm *U9, F1*
(to) **watch television** fernsehen *U3, M*
water sports Wassersport *U6, M*
way Weg *U1, F3;* (to) **ask the way** nach dem Weg fragen *U11, F3;* (to) **be on your way** unterwegs sein *U1, F3;* **by the way** übrigens *U1, M*
(to) **wear** *(Kleidung)* tragen *U11, M*
weather Wetter *U8, F2*
wedding Hochzeit *U3, F2*
Wednesday Mittwoch *U6, F1*
week Woche *U1, S;* **weekend** Wochenende *U2, F2*
(to) **weigh** wiegen *U8, F1*
welcome (to) willkommen (bei) *U1, M*
well nun, na ja *U3, F2;* **well** *Adverb von* good *U3, F2;* **well-known** sehr bekannt *U9, F2*
west West-, westlich *U6, F2*
wet nass, feucht *U8, M*
what was *U1, F3;* **What about ... ?** Was ist mit ... ? *U4, F2;* **What else?** Was noch? *U12, F3;* **What kind of ... ?** Was für ein/e ... ? *U6, F2;* **What sort of ...?** was für (ein/e) ...? *U10, F1*
wheel Rad *U7, F1*
when wenn; als; wann *U2, S*
where wo, woher *U1, M;* wohin *U5, F2*
which welche/r/s *U1, F3*
whisky Whisky *U4, F1*
white weiß *U10, M*
who wer *U3, F1*
whole ganze/r/s *U9, F2*
why warum *U5, F2*
wife Ehefrau *U3, F2*
wild wild *U8, F1*
wilderness Wildnis *U8, F2*
will werden *U8, M*
window Fenster *U6, S*
wine Wein *U2, S;* **wine shop** Weinhandlung *U2, S*
winter Winter *U5, F3;* **winter holiday** Winterurlaub *U8, F2*
(to) **wish** wünschen *U8, M*
with mit *U2, F1*
without ohne *U8, S*
woman, women Frau, Frauen *U7, F2*
wonderful wunderbar *U3, M*
word Wort *U1, F2;* **word order** Wortstellung *U12, F3;* **word spider** Wortnetz *U1, F2*
work Arbeit *U2, F2;* (to) **be at work** auf/bei der Arbeit sein *U2, F2;* (to) **work late** lange arbeiten *U12, F2;* (to) **work out** (hart) trainieren *U6, F2*
worker Arbeiter/in *U5, F3*
working day Arbeitstag *U5, F2*
world Welt *U4, F1*
(to) **worry** sich Sorgen machen *U3, F2;* (to) **be worried** besorgt/beunruhigt sein *U9, S*
worse *Komparativ von* bad, schlechter *U9, F1*
wouldn't *verneinte Form von* would *U11, F1*
(to) **write** schreiben *U1, F2;* (to) **write down** aufschreiben, notieren *U6, F2*
writer Schriftsteller/in *U2, M*
wrong falsch *U1, F3;* **wrong number** falsch verbunden *U1, F3*
www World Wide Web *U2, F2*

Y, y
year Jahr *U2, M*
yellow gelb *U10, M*
yes ja *U1, F3*
yesterday gestern *U7, F1*
you Sie, dich, euch *U1, F1*
young jung *U7, M*
your Ihr, dein, euer/eure *U1, F1*
yourself dich (selbst) *U1, F1*

Z, z
zero Null *U8, F1*
zoo Zoo *U6, F2*